FRESH
FAITH

Other books by Sarah Coleman Kelnhofer:
Changing Lives
God Who?
Stories From Beyond the Edge, editor

To order, call 1-800-765-6955.
Visit us at www.reviewandherald.com for information on other
Review and Herald products.

SARAH COLEMAN KELNHOFER, EDITOR

YOUNG ADULT DEVOTIONAL

FRESH___
FAITH

ℛ

REVIEW AND HERALD® PUBLISHING ASSOCIATION
HAGERSTOWN, MD 21740

The author assumes full responsibility for the accuracy of all facts
and quotations as cited in this book.

Texts credited to Clear Word are from *The Clear Word,* copyright © 1994 by
Jack J. Blanco.
Texts credited to NIV are from the *Holy Bible, New International Version.*
Copyright © 1973, 1978, 1984, International Bible Society. Used by permission of
Zondervan Bible Publishers.
Texts credited to NKJV are from the New King James Version. Copyright ©
1979, 1980, 1982 by Thomas Nelson, Inc. Used by permission. All rights reserved.

This book was
Edited by Andy Nash
Copyedited by Lori Halvorsen and James Cavil
Designed by Tina M. Ivany
Cover designed by Saschane Stephenson
Electronic makeup by Shirley M. Bolivar
Cover art by Tony Stone
Typeset: Usherwood 11/14

PRINTED IN U.S.A.

05 04 03 02 01   5 4 3 2 1

R&H Cataloging Service
Fresh faith. Sarah Coleman Kelnhofer, ed.

    1. Seventh-day Adventists—Doctrines.   2. Young adults—Prayer books and
devotions.   3. College students—Prayer books and devotions.
I. Kelnhofer, Sarah Coleman, ed.

                         286.732

ISBN 0-8280-1599-6

DEDICATION

For the 26 big thinkers, who shared their convictions here;
AND
For our fellow seekers, whose thoughts we hope to challenge.

CONTENTS _____

INTRODUCTION _____

L ast week I attended a Saturday night service at Calvary Chapel in Albuquerque, New Mexico. My husband and I stood for the song service (along with at least 1,000 other people) and mouthed the words to the song a bleached-blond guitarist introduced.

"He's changed hair color again," the woman ahead of us whispered to her companion, and I smiled discreetly. Only in this generation would a church leader feel free to experiment radically with his hair *and* keep a position on the podium. Thirty years ago that would have been taboo.

As the praise song continued, I mulled over the many other facets of Christianity that have changed with time. When my parents attended church together as newlyweds, nobody had thought of projecting song lyrics onto 12-foot screens at the front of the sanctuary. Power Point was unheard of. And, in my home church, at least, no one dared to mention the four-letter word: *drum.* Now, these things and more are commonplace in many churches across the country.

I concluded that our approach to church, spirituality, and religion has changed to reflect society's progress. We want our faith to keep up with the fast-paced world around us; we display a low tolerance for the "plodders" who insist on maintaining generations-old traditions. "Time to move on," we fuss. "Time to embrace the future."

But while progress is good, some things should be left alone. For example, the basis of our faith will never change. "Jesus Christ is the same yesterday and today and forever" (Hebrews 13:8, NIV). "Let us fix our eyes on Jesus, the author and perfecter of our faith" (Hebrews 12:2, NIV).

While *we* may view Jesus in new or electrifying ways, *He* hasn't changed a bit. The God of the universe (and His holy Word) should always constitute the moral center of our universe. While hairstyles, praise music, and witnessing approaches may evolve through the years, the core of Christianity *can never change.*

God is the ruler of the universe, and His Word is infallible, "God-breathed" (2 Timothy 3:16, NIV), and relevant. Accept these two statements, and you've established the basis for the same faith Marrtin Luther, the founder of Protestantism, discovered 500 years ago.

But what about doctrine? Even Martin Luther had to progress past the first basic truths. How does an enlightened inhabitant of the twenty-first century balance unchanging truth with personal study and interpretation? And where does the process begin?

That's where this book comes in.

Here, you'll find 27 young adults who have struggled with tough questions and reached resolution in their own lives. You'll find the proof—*real* proof from a Bible that cannot lie—that helped them form conclusions. And you'll find questions to help you sort out your beliefs as you go along.

It's quite a nice package, really. No, it's not an exhaustive work of research (see the appendix for a reference to that) but it will provide you with a springboard for finding a faith that works for you. I hope, as you read, that each story comes alive for you and leads you closer to the Saviour, Jesus Christ. May this book help you (as it did me) to become even more grounded in your Christianity—"rooted and built up in him," (Colossians 2:7, NIV), and eager to share your new, fresh faith with others.

—Sarah Coleman Kelnhofer

1

THE WORD OF GOD
Harold Zapata

Why Should I Care?

Understanding and hearing the Word of God will give me a basis for a right Christian life.

How Can I Know?

2 Peter 1:20, 21

2 Timothy 3:16, 17

Psalm 119:105

Proverbs 30:5, 6

Isaiah 8:20

John 17:17

1 Thessalonians 2:13

Hebrews 4:12

John 1:1-3, 14

Hebrews 1:1

Romans 15:4

Psalm 138:2

Job 23:12

Isaiah 40:8

John 5:39

Acts 17:11

Hebrews 1:3

1 Peter 1:23

Luke 4:32

Luke 8:11

Colossians 3:16

John 15:3

Psalm 119:9

Jeremiah 15:16

Matthew 4:4

Hebrews 6:5

"Thy word have I hid in mine heart, that I might not sin against thee" (Psalm 119:11).

Great beads of sweat cascaded down my weary face, back, and legs as the hot summer sun melted away all my intensity and desire to keep selling Bibles house to house. About 2:00 p.m. I found myself in a barrio—downtown Los Angeles. Boom boxes played in yellow low-riders and little tots splashed in blue plastic Wal-Mart pools in their fenced front yards as I was walked—feeling led by the Spirit—to a little yellow two-story apartment. I proceeded to the second story, apartment 9.

The number was hanging for its life from a blue tack as I knocked on the faded brown door. I saw the curtains move behind the window next to the door. I knocked again, and now saw a pair of big friendly eyes behind the curtains. As I knocked a third time, she opened the door. *Naked!*

"Come in," the beautiful woman invited softly. Echoes of warning rushed into my head. "Flee youthful lusts! Flee youthful lusts! Flee youthful lusts!" pounded its way into my heart. I looked to my left and ran. Then I ran some more. I felt like that young lawyer in his dark-blue suit and purple briefcase fleeing from "the firm."

Finally catching my breath three blocks later, I realized I had forgotten something at the foot of Jezebel's door. My briefcase! I had left all my Bibles at the entrance to Hotel California. What was I supposed to do?

I slowly approached the gateway to death, that brown door with the hanging number 9. From a distance I could see that she had left the bait just outside her door, opening the curtain or the door every so often to see if her victim would return.

I made a run for it: Up the stairs, down the hall—I snatched the suitcase full of Bibles as I zoomed past her door. I fled temptation and never left a forwarding address.

That suitcase held more than just a stash of valuable books. The Bible doesn't contain the Word of God; the Bible *is* the Word of God. This Book we hold in our hands is the living, breathing, invigorating Word of a personal and loving God. It reveals who He is, His personality and thoughts, His desires and purposes. The Bible reveals what He can do in light of what He has done. Through the recorded ups and downs of God's relationship with individuals and a nation called Israel, we find valuable lessons for us in these last days.

God inspired holy people of old with His thoughts, and they in turn wrote them in their own languages, according to their culture and education. However, while Moses wrote, God added Spirit to the ink and life to the printed word. While David strummed his harp, God strummed the cords of his heart—David's melodies of salvation and praise give witness to that truth. While Solomon spoke, God directed his lips and made the preacher eloquent. Though penned by people, the Word is from God Himself.

And where the Word of the King is, there is power. It was by His Word that the Lord made the heavens and all the host of them. The same power that created the universe is available to re-create the person that walks in the light of His Word. All things are sustained by the power of His Word—marriages, nations, churches, businesses, hopes, and dreams. There is nothing that cannot be transformed when put under the light of God's Word. The power of God's Holy Word converts the foolish into wise, changes the timid into bold, and makes the weak strong.

To be honest, I used to think the Bible was a boring book. I thought it had nothing really important to say to me. I didn't realize then that spiritual things must be spiritually discerned (see 1 Corinthians 2:14). One day in Germany, as I was about to purchase another pack of cigarettes, I heard a voice behind me say, "Harold, I can't help you like that." I immediately turned around, but there was no one behind me. I shook it off and proceeded to purchase the cigarettes when again the voice said: "Harold, I can't help you like that." For the first time in my life, I realized that there was a living God who knew me by name. I looked up to heaven, and I lost the strength of my legs. I wanted a smoke so badly! I began to cry. When I finally got up, I left the addicted Harold in the street and began a new life in Christ. Would you believe it? God took the craving away from me that very same hour. This spiritual experience helped me discern the fingerprint of God in His Holy Word. Now I'm not just reading the Bible; I'm actually loving it!

When I got back home after my encounter with the seductress, I looked at my one remaining Bible, and I said to myself: "Self, today you *saved your Bible.*" Then I paused and smiled as I chuckled: "No, rather my *Bible saved me!*"

1. So, what's up with you and your Bible? Can you listen to God talking to you?
2. Have any of God's promises helped you in times of danger, temptation, or fear?
3. Has the Word of God transformed an area of your life? If so, which one?
4. What different choices would you make if you spent 20 minutes a day reading God's Word? Where could you be in one year's time?
5. Are you too busy to hear God?
6. What priority does God's Holy Word have in your life?

Harold Zapata, 29, is the senior pastor of the Central Seventh-day Adventist Church in Albuquerque, New Mexico. He is the husband of one inspiring wife, Evelyn, and the proud dad of two angels, Natalie, 5, and Jasmine, 2. He still daydreams about scoring the winning goal for the U.S. team in the World Cup.

2

THE GODHEAD
Brenda Keller Janzen

Why Should I Care?

A God made up of three beings is unexplainable yet reassuring, because all three are working together in perfect, loving harmony for my redemption.

How Can I Know?

Deuteronomy 6:4

Matthew 28:19

2 Corinthians 13:14

Ephésians 4:4-6

1 Peter 1:2

1 Timothy 1:17

Revelation 14:7

Galatians 4:6

Acts 2:17

1 Corinthians 1:9

Hebrews 1:3

Luke 22:69

John 3:16-18

Mom, what is God like?" I asked, wrapping my chubby 6-year-old fingers around her thumb.

"Well, there are lots of things to learn. First of all, He is actually three, a Trinity that—"

"But Mom, how can three people fit into one person?"

"Well, it's not *quite* like that, sweetie," Mom chuckled, tucking the covers under my chin. "You see, God the Father, God the Son, and God the Holy Spirit are separate, yet they're each part of the Godhead."

"OK, I think I get it. It's like He goes by three different names. Like how I use my first name, my last name, and my nickname, right?"

"Well . . . sort of, but God really is three different Beings. Yet God is one."

"Um, I don't understand."

"I know, hon," Mom said patiently. "Right now we can't understand everything about God, but someday you can ask Him to explain it to you personally. So for now, let's go to sleep, OK?"

The routine was familiar. A notoriously inquisitive child, I *had* to have answers. And bedtime often served as my learning lab. Tonight's topic especially baffled me. How could God be three, but at the same time be one? I just couldn't think about it for long without going totally bonkers.

Finally, on one of those sleepless nights, I hit on the perfect Godhead metaphor. I decided He was like a three-way mirror—when you look into one you see three different parts of the same subject. A "three-in-one" God. That seemed like a very good explanation, and my young heart was satisfied.

My childhood faith was strong, simple. But as I entered my teenage years, I started to grapple with my beliefs about God. To question, not for the sake of discovering pat answers, but to really know *why* I believed in Him, to know *what* I believed about Him.

During our boarding school years my friend Jen and I often conducted late-night Bible discussions after lights out. Sitting cross-legged on Jen's bed, flashlights beaming at our open Bibles, we'd battle it out.

"So, how is it that 'God is Love' " (1 John 4:8), I asked one night, "when I read texts like this: 'The Lord, the God of Israel, says: "Each man strap a sword to his side. Go back and forth through the camp . . . , each killing his brother and friend and neighbor"' (Exodus 32:27, NIV)?"

"Maybe they needed to be punished. Did you read the whole context?"

"But Jen, do you really get that passage? God actually asked people to go out and *murder* their own relatives!"

Jen shrugged.

"And what about this one?" I aimed my flashlight at another passage and fired away. "'That night I will go through the land and every firstborn male of both men and animals will die'" (Exodus 12:12, Clear Word).

"In that case it seems to me that God was proving a really big point. He needed everyone to recognize that He was the only God of the universe, and that—"

"But what loving God would kill innocent animals and babies to prove a point?" I interrupted. "And He's the author of the Ten Commandments, which tell us that murder is wrong. I just don't get it."

Jen tucked the flashlight up under her chin and scowled in the eerie glow. "OK, what is this, the Inquisition? Is God on trial here? What's up?"

"Well . . . I guess I'm just having trouble making all of the pieces fit," I admitted, jabbing a fist into Jen's pillow. "This harsh-sounding God doesn't seem to match the merciful, loving one I find in other parts of the Bible."

"I know, I know," she sighed.

So we kept searching. Kept praying for peace, for understanding.

Several nights and many passages later we landed on a promising verse: "I want you to have the same inner peace that I have—not the kind of peace that the world gives, but that abiding peace with the Father that only I can give. Don't be afraid of Him, because He loves you" (John 14:27, Clear Word).

"I like that," said Jen. "What do you think?"

"Hmm, well . . . it sounds comforting," I mused. "It does seem clear that through Christ we can really connect with the Father."

Occasionally I'd come across other texts that helped solve the mystery of God. But it was like trying to work an intricately complex jigsaw puzzle—although sometimes a couple pieces would snap into place, more often I concentrated on the many missing pieces. Frustrated, I continued my spiritual exploration.

Several years later the three-in-one God topic again came into sharp focus. I had been asked to write a story for young readers, illustrating God's roles. As I sat staring at a blank computer screen, I prayed, "God, I need to hear from You, to be directed by Your Spirit—after all, this story is about You. Please be here and guide me." Taking a deep breath, I opened the Word, but this time I began in the New Testament.

As I read I realized that not until the birth of Christ were the distinct yet harmonious roles of the Godhead for this earth fully revealed. As the angel explained to Mary: "The Holy Spirit will come upon you, and the power of the Most High will overshadow you. So the holy one to be born will be called the Son of God" (Luke 1:35, NIV). The beautifully intertwined roles suddenly stood out: the Father gave His Son, Christ gave Himself, and the Spirit gave Jesus His earthly form. The more time I spent learning about this divine Trio, the more fascinated I became.

That writing assignment triggered a lasting renewal of my interest in the Godhead. As my spiritual quest has continued, I still marvel at the profound simplicity of the God I discovered as a child. At the same time I'm fascinated by the unexplainable complexity of the God I encountered during my teenage years. My adult faith is a combination of my childhood's simple trust and my youth's searching instinct, merged with the mature realization that my earthly mind will never fully comprehend the Godhead mystery. He doesn't expect me to.

So what does God ask of me? Jesus puts it simply in John 14:1: "Do not let your hearts be troubled. Trust in God; trust also in me" (NIV). Even though I cannot completely understand His ways, I am to trust Him. Although He sometimes seems far away from my day-to-day existence, trust. When my dreams lie in pieces, trust that my future rests in the infinitely capable hands of an all-powerful, all-knowing, ever-present God.

My newfound faith in the Godhead is still strong and simple, yet reaching. And these days my search is driven by a deeper motive: to know Him. To build my side of the bridge of friendship with three Beings so closely united in purpose that They *are* one. I'm intrigued by the perfect part each plays in securing my salvation: God the Father, the source of all love, giving the sacrifice of His Son. God the Son, providing the bodily sacrifice, grace for my dark, sinful self.

God the Holy Spirit, the one who whispers into my mind, gently brushing my consciousness with the beauty of the Father's heart, drawing me toward the perfect love Christ poured out for me.

When I get to heaven, the first thing I want to do is meet my three-in-one God. I'll fall and worship at His feet, burst into songs of praise with the vast angel choir, and begin building a one-on-one friendship with my Creator.

But I have a feeling that somewhere along the way, we'll share a déjà-vu moment. Still the inquisitive daughter bursting with a dizzying array of questions, I'll stand face to face with my ultimate Parent. And I'll get to ask Him anything I want . . . including how one Being can exist in three parts.

1. How has your concept of the Godhead changed through the years?

2. Have you wondered about the harshness of God in the Old Testament, as compared to the loving God that Christ portrays in the New Testament?

3. Are you satisfied with your relationship with God? In what ways would you like it to grow and develop?

4. What do you think it will be like to meet each member of the Godhead in person?

5. What is your understanding of the roles that each of Them play?

6. Which one of the Godhead is easiest for you to relate to? Which is most difficult? Why do you think this is?

7. How would you explain the Godhead to someone?

Brenda Keller Janzen, 29, lives near Chattanooga, Tennessee, with her husband, Barry, and two energetic canines, Kato and Kali. She enjoys traveling, brainstorming about heaven, exploring the Internet, and e-friends (you can reach her at bjanzen@mailcity.com).

3

GOD THE FATHER
Gavin Anthony

Why Should I Care?

When I realize that God is actually my Father, He becomes tangible—someone I can touch and truly love.

How Can I Know?

Deuteronomy 32:6	2 Timothy 1:2
Isaiah 64:8	Philippians 4:20
1 Corinthians 8:6	Ephesians 4:4-6
Ephesians 3:14, 15	2 Corinthians 11:31a
Galatians 4:6	Romans 8:15
Jude 1	Psalm 89:26
1 John 3:1	Psalm 103:13
1 John 2:13	Isaiah 63:16

I was kneeling on a freezing cold stone floor with the winter wind blowing through a glassless window when my understanding of God changed forever.

I was working briefly in Albania just after Communism had fallen. Visiting evangelists had baptized the first members of our new church community, and they needed someone to care for them until a full-time minister could arrive. I rearranged my last year at Newbold College (a Christian college in England) and headed out.

It was a most astonishing time. I was one of the first Westerners into the country, and people were just beginning to share their stories of what it had been like to live under a terrible dictator—a dictator who was even counseled by Stalin to ease up on his people. I listened as story after story tumbled out, often on a cascade of bitter tears. Once, we were watching television when the ex-dictator's picture was shown. Instinctively my host shot out of his seat and bent over to within inches of the screen, shouting and shaking his fist angrily at the face. It was understandable. His relatives had been persecuted and even killed for their faith.

It was personally also a very hard time. Night after night I would lie in my bed bewildered by the people's unique and passionate mixture of anger, guilt, betrayal, and hopelessness. I was in Albania to listen, but most important to lead. To guide the people on a journey away from the hurts of the past, to forgiveness, reconciliation, and friendship with the God I had chosen to pursue for the rest of my life.

But how? I was a young free Westerner. What did I know? To make matters worse, there was no one around to help me with the answers. The telephone lines, my one lifeline to the outside world and support, were rarely working. It was just me and, well, God.

I began to pray as I had never prayed before. Not because I had suddenly been convicted of the power of prayer. No, my reason was not that noble. I simply had no other options. "Dear God," I would begin. And then there would be times when I just didn't know what to say. It was all much too big to get my head around.

I was kneeling by my bed one day, going through the "Dear God, I'm desperate again" routine, when suddenly something happened. I don't know why or how it happened, and it didn't really matter then. But as I was kneeling on that cold stone floor, somewhat confused, facedown into my duvet, I realized tht God was my Father.

I wish I could convey what this really means to me. I'm typing these words on my trusty laptop, but am frustrated because I so badly want you capture that encounter. In that briefest of moments God became my Father. He became so real I felt I could touch Him. Even now when I lie in bed at night, I sometimes reach my hand out into the darkness, expecting to touch Him.

In that moment my understanding of the One who rules the universe moved from a label, "God," to a revolutionary encounter, "my Father." Christians can have a very clinical discussion about God. But this becomes impossible if He is your Father.

Imagine being an orphan your whole life. You have never met nor even heard of your father. One day the doorbell rings. You open the door to see an unfamiliar man standing there. He smiles and says, "I'm your father." I think there are only two ways we would react. Our mouths would hang open in amazement, and with tears of joy we would embrace, or else we would slam the door in his face and run back into the house, terrified.

But we could not remained unmoved by this event. The idea that we have a Father in heaven is revolutionary. It is revolutionary because it is so confrontational. This Person claims not only to know us, but to be related to us. And that has countless implications. We can try to run from all this, but we cannot make it untrue.

When we study the Ruler of our universe at school or college, there is always the danger of describing our Father with big theological words—such as "omniscient." While these kinds of descriptions may be true, we can find ourselves keeping God mysterious and distant. But if God is our Father, it's a whole different story!

When I was working with a group of 10- to 14-year-olds in Iceland, I asked them to draw a picture of God, the first person of the Trinity. After finishing, they held up their pictures and described them. I was startled. Each one had included a heart somewhere in their picture. God the Father, they told me emphatically, is love.

"But what about the terrible things we see in the world?" I countered. "All the pain and suffering that we see night after night on the news?"

They wouldn't budge. No matter what the situation was in the world, they were adamant that God is, most of all, a God of love.

I've thought a lot about that experience. Sometime soon after age 14 we begin to rethink who and what God is. We used to be clear about it all, but as life gets increasingly complicated so, it appears, does God. But the secret of these young Icelanders was that they believed a truth about God the Father that was not based on experiences in the world, but on the revelation of our Father in the Bible. They were hanging on to God's words at all costs. Nothing, no matter how horrendous or astonishing, can change His promises. This touchable Father of mine loves me—the Bible tells me so.

Coupled to this is a second truth that I find so wonderful. Since leaving college, I have kept a journal. I wanted to know how God speaks to us, so I logged my discoveries. After six years of writing I was sitting on my bed one evening when I realized rather suddenly, indeed quite abruptly, that my journey was over. It dawned on me that I was asking the wrong question.

For in one way, it really doesn't matter how God speaks, because He is with me. Right here. Right now. If my Father needs to speak, He cannot be in a better place. So in the silence I will sit contented. At peace.

I always remember a friend at college saying, "When God seems far away, who has moved?" I have. If I long to be with Him, I simply need to pause and remember that I *can* be—whenever I choose.

God is my Father. My Father is love. He is with me now. And every "now," forever. The tricky thing is not simply to know this with my head, but to be confronted and revolutionized by this in my heart. A blinding flash of the obvious, if you like.

Why does my Father love me? And why does He come to live, dwell, tabernacle, hang out with me? I find this so shocking, for I don't really see much reason for Him to make the effort. Yet it is precisely *because* there appears no reason for Him to love me and be with me that I find myself so inextricably drawn to Him, longing to touch Him.

I can't help loving a God like this. He's my Father.

1. Do you know the Father more with your head or with your heart?
2. What labels have you given God that actually obscure Him, rather than making Him more real?
3. Make a list of the characteristics of a good earthly father. How similar is your heavenly Father?
4. Sometimes our earthly fathers can be quite the opposite of God.

How would you show who has had a bad experience with their father that our Father in heaven can be trusted?

5. How would you draw a picture of your Father in heaven?

6. If you want to know your Father in heaven better than you do right now, what are you going to do next?

7. When was the last time you reached out and touched your Father?

Gavin Anthony, 33, wrote this from a small village on the south coast of England. One day he will reach out his hand again, and it really will touch the Father's.

4

GOD THE SON
Julie Z. Lee

Why Should I Care?
The reality of Jesus' sacrifice and love can exist in our efforts to achieve good.

How Can I Know?

John 1:1-3, 14	Luke 1:35
Colossians 1:15-19	Philippians 2:5-11
John 10:30; 14:9	Hebrews 2:9-18
Romans 6:23	1 Corinthians 15:3, 4
2 Corinthians 5:17-19	Hebrews 8:1, 2
John 5:22	John 14:1-3

The summer I visited Italy, I saw Christ.

Marble Christ, stained-glass Christ, and metal sculpture Christ. Oil-based acrylic, and even fabric Christ. Christ on a cross, Christ standing up, Christ lying down, Christ walking around. One hundred and one ways to depict Jesus—the miracle worker, the revolutionary, the Saviour, a god who died for our sins—the God. He is the ultimate work of art, sensational in the genius of Michaelangelo's hands, a legend we tell to our children and ourselves. Framed in gold, guarded by rails, covered by glass—permittable for sight but not for touch . . . for touch will deteriorate Him.

This was my Jesus.

✦ ✦ ✦

Months before my wedding I was talking on the phone with my grandmother. Needless to say, there were hundreds of details to discuss. After conferences on flowers, cakes, photographers, and dresses, I raised a topic that had concerned me ever since my engagement.

"How will we pay for this?" I asked my grandmother. I was raised by a single mother, so fiscal matters were always a primary issue.

"Don't worry," she replied. "Your mother will take care of it."

"But how? How will she afford it?"

Again my grandmotehr reassured me.

But stubborn and curious, I persisted, refusing the faith she was urging me to take. "Please tell me how!"

My grandmother became angry. "Do you think your mother is a fool? Your mother has been preparing for this day for a long time! She works hard to provide for you. Do not doubt her when you have always gone without want."

I stopped questioning the matter out loud.

Weeks later I noticed my mother and grandmother exchanging glances and mumbling brief words. My mother then left the room, returning minutes later with a standard letter-sized envelope. It was thick, heaving at its flimsy, folded seams. She handed it to me.

"What is this?" I asked, carefully lifting the flap.

The envelope contained a large stack of bills. My eyes grew wide, then looked up at my mother.

"Have you ever held that much money in your hands?" she asked solemnly.

"Never."

"It's all yours. Deposit it into your account and use it to pay for everything regarding the wedding. It's everything you will need."

With the accessibility of electronic transfers and checking accounts, I wondered why my mother did not opt for something more guarded than this free wielding of cash. The thought of carrying around so much value frightened me.

"Why didn't you just write me a check?"

"I wanted you to hold it. I wanted you to feel what it's like to hold that much money in your hands."

We sat there for a moment: I, the recipient of the means to begin a new life, and she, the giver.

❖ ❖ ❖

The woman pushes through the crowds of Jerusalem, her body weak with the monotony of long-term illness. Before her—between the arms, legs, torsos—walks (no, not just the illusion of!) hope. She needs to touch Him, only grasp a corner of His existence to understand reality as He promises to give.

She reaches.

Rough fabric bristles against her fingertips, leaving a coat of dust from where the robe has dragged along dirt roads traveled. The pungent smell of journey engulfs her, and she hears a voice asking who has touched Him. Someone is touching her. Christ and she, no longer apart. Realizing they never were.

❖ ❖ ❖

Marble Christ, stained-glass Christ, oil-based, acrylic, and even fabric Christ. Framed in gold, guarded by rails, covered by glass— permittable for sight but not for touch . . . touch will deteriorate Him.

The illusion of Jesus.

I used to believe that Christ was inaccessible, bogged with antiquity, separated from us by sky, heaven, and centuries of time. I found Him outdated and His method of communication too taxing. It was easier to keep Him behind the glass that preserved His perfection rather than make Him a real part of me. I didn't see how His famous life could be relevant to my own. Abstract theories and fantastic legends of the Bible—they had no real place in my heart.

I remember nights I used to pray that Jesus might make Himself tangible to me. I would speak out loud, hoping to meet some reply, a manifestation of divine conversation (a ray of moonlight, growling thunder, the glowing apparition of Jesus Himself?)—anything that signified His presence in my life.

Instead I got silence. It would break me, this silence—this empty response. Pained by years spent straining my ears only to hear nothing, I pleaded that I had better not be "talking to the walls."

Just talking to the walls after all these years.

Spans of walls, miles of sky, centuries of living and dying—all coming between me and everyone's Jesus.

Then, strangely enough, I began to meet Christ. On the streets, in the classroom, in the office, in the home. I saw that He wears not the unapproachable robes of divinity but the rugged garments of a carpenter, a teacher, a friend, a mother. He travels not by luminous light but upon the straps of dusty sandals, finding rest in fishermen's boats. He drives an old minivan to and from duties, working long hours to feed me, clothe me, care for me. He silently makes sacrifices for my life. He asks that I hold in my hand what it means to love. What it means to sacrifice so that I may begin a new life. To smell, taste, hear, see, and touch the raw of humanity and know what it means to be human.

Centuries ago God sent His only begotten Son, not to boast or encase Him in glass, but so that Jesus could be touched by the bleeding fingers of our existence. To touch us back. He came not to become a legend, a mythological figure, an icon to behold and only behold, but to become human.

God, our Father, could have written us a check to expedite the process of our salvation, but He wanted us to know what it was like to hold His love in our hands. To have Jesus live among us.

Has this tangible part of Jesus faded with time? Is He no longer human enough to hold?

No. Touching Jesus is just a matter of shattering the glass we've placed Him behind.

Through the power of our heavenly Father, Jesus Christ's humanity, love, sacrifice—the capacity of all these things that embody Him—can exist in us. The reality of Jesus can be here. Perhaps in glimpses. Perhaps only in short episodes, gritty with the dust of life, but never closed off. Never just a work of art. Never an illusion.

The reality of Jesus eats, sleeps, and breathes in our potential for goodness. In our greatest moments we see Jesus in each other—a Jesus we can smell, hear, and touch—without consequences and without deterioration.

He works in you, in me.
This is Jesus.

1. Is it vital to your spirituality to know that the life of Jesus on earth was real? Or are His teachings enough to sustain your beliefs?
2. Do you think that during Jesus' time on earth He experienced all the emotional joys and pains a human can have? Would it make a difference in your faith if He did or did not?
3. How human do you think we can allow Jesus to become in our minds without diminishing our reverence for Him?
4. What is the relevance of God's decision to have Jesus become a human and die for our salvation? Do you think it was the only option?
5. Jesus is the physical manifestation of God's nature. How does this affect your relationships with God and Jesus? Does it enhance your understanding of God?
6. Does the distinction between God and Jesus make a difference in your spiritual life?
7. If we all have the potential to reflect the nature of Jesus in ourselves, what changes does that prompt you to make in your own life?

Julie Z. Lee, 24, lives with her best friend and husband, Milbert Mariano, in Angwin, California, where they both work at Pacific Union College. Along with cooking, writing, and reading, she also tolerates occasional exercise in the form of hiking and biking in the woods near her home—but only when the weather is pleasant and the trail is void of strenuous hills.

5

GOD THE HOLY SPIRIT

Cory Wetterlin

Why Should I Care?

We will understand God the Holy Spirit when we come near to Him by studying His personhood, calling for us, gifts for us, messages for the world, and meaning in our personal lives. When the Spirit comes near, He will be real.

How Can I Know?

Calling
Acts1:8; 2:1-4; 9:17; 13:2
Ephesians 4:11, 12
Judges 6:34; 11:29; 13:25
1 Samuel 10:10; 16:13
Isaiah 11:2; 61:1
Matthew 1:18; 3:16; 4:1

Personhood
Ephesians 4:30
Psalm 106:33; 139:7
Isaiah 63:10
Matthew 12:31
Acts 5:3
Hebrews 10:29

Messages
John 15:26; 16:7-14
2 Samuel 23:2
Revelation 2:7

Gifts
Romans 5:5
Galatians 5:22; 6:8
1 Corinthians 2:14
Exodus 31:3
Joel 2:28
John 6:63
Romans 8:23, 26
2 Peter 1:21
Jude 20

Identity   *Assurance*
John 14:16, 17, 26   Romans 8:14, 16
                                    2 Corinthians 1:22
                                    1 John 3:24
                                    Psalm 51:11

When I was 6 or 7 my parents decided that we were going to go visit my grandmother in California. I don't remember much about the trip, except that we were going to go to Disneyland. I hadn't thought that I would ever go. In fact, it seemed so far away that I didn't consider it as a possibility. It wasn't real to me yet. And even as we went down to California I didn't think about it much. But the night before, in the hotel, you better believe I started to think about it!

I have a habit (which was overpronounced when I younger) of rubbing my hands together when I get excited about something. But that night, the night before Disneyland, my dad tells me that I was so pumped up that not only was I rubbing my palms together, but my childish hands were moving across the full length of my arms and my legs while I was sleeping. I was either really wound up or really cold.

The look in my eyes when I woke removed all doubt—I was definitely energized. It was when Disneyland finally became real that I got excited about it.

Disneyland was not real to me when it was far away, and neither is God the Holy Spirit when He seems to be far away.

I was raised as a fine upstanding Christian boy. I went to Christian grade schools, a Christian academy, and Christian colleges. When I got to academy, I found myself looking at God as someone whom I believed in. I knew He was out there somewhere, but I also felt that He was not directly involved in my life. I got a taste of His presence in my activities on drama ministry teams from my senior year of academy through my sophomore year of college, which made me wonder if there was something more to His power. But I still did not experience God until I began the next adventure in my life, YouthNet eXtreme.

YouthNet eXtreme is a national touring youth evangelism team, and I got a chance to be part of its first year of ministry. The team took a group of college students equipped with the gifts of music, drama, speaking, sound, and lighting, put them in a truck, and sent them across the country to share their faith with other college students and youth. And although the year I spent on the team was an amazing success, it still took some time to get used to the whole idea.

I remember walking out into the cool Maryland air early on a June morning in 1998. I had begun to realize this adventure that I had signed up for was not just a weeklong drama tour or even a three-month summer camp. This was to be the king of road trips, a full 12 months of travel. I didn't feel prepared for such a journey and didn't understand how I was really going to be able to handle it. I tried so desperately to wrap my own arms around more than my physical body. I needed them to reach inside and comfort my soul.

But neither the sound of twigs nor the grass under my feet nor the peaceful stream running under the footbridge could comfort me. I began to pour out my soul to heaven. I told God of my uncertainty, my excitement, and my need for assurance. And that morning, that cold summer morning in Maryland, I truly met God. I no longer needed my arms to reach inside, for His were already there. From that comfort came strength. From strength came assurance and the acceptance of my call to work on the team.

The rest of the year was filled with experiences that I will never forget and a God who is personal to me. When the Holy Spirit came near, I found that He was real.

It was not until I entered a classroom at Andrews University (a Christian school) that I realized that the God I met that morning was God the Holy Spirit. I had always thought of the Holy Spirit as some vague presence or maybe a communications system to heaven; He was too far away to be real. But I found out that the Holy Spirit is much more than an inanimate object. He can be grieved, angered, rebelled against, sinned against, and lied to (Ephesians 4:30; Psalm 106:33; 139:7; Isaiah 63:10; Matthew 12:31; Acts 5:3; Hebrews

10:29). If you think about it, you can't lie to a chair or grieve a communication system!

When we begin to understand Jesus' promise in John 14-16 that He will send us the Holy Spirit, it becomes clear that He is not just promising a communication system. He is promising part of Himself. He is promising God. This is when we can know that God is close to us and we begin to see Him as real. Suddenly the concept of the Holy Spirit being a comforter makes sense, because we know God is comforting us. The arms that wrapped around me in Maryland were God's arms through another part of Himself: the Holy Spirit. It was also God the Holy Spirit that called me into ministry that year and into the future—bringing a change in my major, from psychology to theology.

Just as the Holy Spirit called the disciples in the book of Acts; Gideon, Jephthah, and Samson in the book of Judges; Saul and David in the book of Samuel; and Mary in the Gospel of Matthew, Christ's call came from the Holy Spirit in the river Jordan. The Bible tells us that it was the Holy Spirit that led Christ into the wilderness.

Not only does the Spirit comfort us and call us; He also gives us the skills to do the work. I did not give the talents of music, drama, and speaking to myself. They were given to me by the Holy Spirit and used by the Holy Spirit (see Exodus 31:3; Joel 2:28). These gifts would have meant nothing without the words to speak. This too is the job of the Holy Spirit: to testify to the truth and remind us of the messages of Christ. We experienced this on YouthNet eXtreme team so many times. We often got up in front of a new group of kids, not knowing what their needs were, but somehow we ended up meeting those needs. Many times our meetings would completely change from what we had planned, and we would find that the Spirit had a reason and a soul to reach.

For me, the missing piece in the puzzle of the Holy Spirit has been filled by gaining understanding of the Holy Spirit: Once I did, I could see Him all over my life. God became real to me throughout the course of my life and the paths that He was directing me to go in. When God the Holy Spirit comes near, He becomes real.

1. Do you agree that the Holy Spirit has a Personhood? Why or why not?
2. Have you been in a situation where the Holy Spirit has provided you with the words to speak?
3. What does it mean to be baptized in the Holy Spirit?
4. How can we pray in the Holy Spirit? (See Jude 20.)
5. What does it mean to sin against the Holy Spirit? (See Matthew 12:31.)
6. In John 16:7-14 we are told that Jesus is not going to tell us everything, but that the Spirit will tell us of things to come. Does this have relevance to some of the issues in the church today that the Bible doesn't seem to be completely clear on?
7. What are the spiritual things that we cannot understand without the Holy Spirit? (See 1 Corinthians 2:14.)

Cory Wetterlin, 22, recently married Laura Whidden and is currently finishing his religion degree. He plans to join a pastoral or evangelistic ministry with an edge. (He's not sure what the edge means right now.)

6

CREATION
Lynette Roberts Lounsbury

Why Should I Care?

Believing in creation provides me with a unique relationship with God. My view of my environment and myself changes when I realize I was handmade by a God who cares.

How Can I Know?

Exodus 20:11

Genesis 1:1-31

Psalm 33:6-9

Hebrews 11:3

Genesis 2:4-25

John 1:1-3

Ephesians 3:9

Hebrews 1:2

Revelation 13:8

Psalm 19:1-4

1 Corinthians 11:9

Genesis 2:20

Romans 1:20

1 Chronicles 16:24-27

Psalm 96:5, 6

I have always loved magazines—fashion, beauty, health, sport, current affairs, photography. You name it—I'll be enthralled by it (as long as there are pictures!). I love the color and the beautiful people and scenes. I always thought it would be an exciting job to work for, or model for, a magazine. Perhaps the phony perfection created within the pages appealed to me.

I got my chance during my first year of college. A tall, well-dressed man came up to me on the street and asked me if I'd ever considered modeling. As most people would agree, flattery is blinding—and it wasn't long before I was nervously entering the slick headquarters of his agency for a "look-see." I was studying hard for my literature degree, but in those few moments the most important thing to me was what they thought of the way I looked. He offered to shoot me a portfolio of photographs, and for a few days I was living every college girl's fantasy.

But like any feeling that is based on external perceptions, it waned rapidly. My body image was totally destroyed by a few months in an industry I will never again admire. I had never thought of dieting before, and I had never even heard of "cellulite"! Nothing like that had mattered in high school. Despite my small frame, I was called "voluptuous" and asked to consider losing weight to get more work. I was sent to castings where the girls were so critical of each other that they were openly derogatory and cruel. I saw young girls in tears because television producers bluntly told them they looked fat on screen. Very soon I started to feel like an unattractive, overfed piece of meat—as though every time someone glanced at me, I was being examined and evaluated.

I failed fairly miserably as a model and left after only six months. I never told anyone how I felt, because it seems such a glamorous industry to most onlookers. I made other excuses and tried to sound aloof. I didn't really want to talk about it for years, and I still struggle with my body image. Looks became more important to me than my character, and I lost much of my innocent self-confidence because of that experience.

I might have always considered that year a terrible experience if I had not been at a worship one night in my college dorm. A friend of mine was speaking, so I had made an effort to attend. Occasionally God gives us an unmistakable message, and that night I heard it in the first words my friend spoke: "Isn't it great that God doesn't look at us the way we do?"

I don't remember anything else that she said that night, but I remember thinking about her words for a long time, about the fact that God saw me as extremely valuable—enough to risk *His* happiness for. It struck me that God took that risk for anyone, not based on whether they were photogenic or not, but on the fact that He had made them and loved them. The phrase in Jeremiah, "Before I formed you in the womb I knew you" (1:5, NIV), reminded me of what I had misunderstood so incredibly: God created me and loved me, and that made me worthwhile. No photograph, opinion, diet, or university degree could ever make me any more important to Him. And with that knowledge came the great relief that I could stop trying to be good enough.

Hours of philosophical study had made me view Creation as merely a mythical, biblical description of evolution, and the idea of God actually forming man out of clay seemed a little trite. But I suddenly realized how important it was to actually believe in a literal Creation. If we don't believe in it, then our looks and actions don't matter, because those things are *all* we are. If we weren't created, if we evolved slowly from a piece of slime, then how can we see ourselves as anything other than sophisticated, well-dressed, highly educated pieces of slime? God molded us out of clay, and that makes us works of art no matter what we look like. That realization made me reevaluate my image of myself, and fortunately it began to matter less what *I* saw and more what God did.

This discovery has also changed the way I look around me. Other people seem more valuable when I realize that God carved them into who they are. He created every facet of their physique and layered them with talents. I realize that the environment we live in is a masterpiece of supernatural design. God created—whether it be in seven literal or figurative days—an entire planet of intricate and symbiotic life. And like "the Force" in *Star Wars,* He endowed it all, including us, with a spirit of life. This knowledge made me rethink my stance on everything from pollution and recycling to vegetarianism.

Today I can look back and laugh at my naïve excursion into a world that has forgotten that we are "fearfully and wonderfully made" (Psalm 139:14). But I cannot laugh at the many people who have forgotten that fact. As a high school teacher I cringe when I see girls as young as 13 and 14 refusing lunch because they need to stay slim—and it happens a lot! I hear kids with amazing academic potential or great ball-handling skills belittling themselves because they don't look like airbrushed superstars. If it makes me sad, imagine the frustration God feels!

A belief in the miracle of Creation has changed my view of both myself and the world I live in. I have become part of an immense and important whole, and I am significant because I have been made by God.

1. How does belief in Creation change your outlook on life?
2. How do you think God wants you to view yourself and the rest of His creation?
3. Does this idea of Creation change the way we should view and treat our environment?
4. Would you feel differently about yourself if you knew you had evolved from a single-celled organism?
5. How do you respond to people who call Creation a myth?
6. Is there a place for the theories of Darwin and evolution?
7. Could you explain your belief in Creation to someone else?

Lynette Roberts Lounsbury, 23, lives with her husband, Jim, in Newcastle, Australia, where she teaches English at Avondale Adventist High School and is still studying literature. She loves exercise and martial arts, but refuses to diet and now models only for her husband!

7

THE NATURE OF MAN
Matthew W. Gamble

Why Should I Care?
Understanding our human nature will enable us to understand why we do the things that we do and to see what Christ can offer us.

How Can I Know?

Genesis 1:26-28

Genesis 2:7, 15

Genesis 3

Psalm 8:4-8

Psalm 51:10

Matthew 5:21, 22

Matthew 6:22, 23

Acts 17:24-28

Romans 5:12-17

Romans 6:12, 13

1 Corinthians 6:19, 20

2 Corinthians 5:19, 20

Galatians 2:20, 21

1 John 4:7, 8, 11, 20

Revelation 3:17

As a child I thought very little about God. I was raised in a Catholic home where we attended church only before an Easter egg hunt or after opening Christmas presents. And although my parents told me what was right and wrong, there were always occasions when I didn't know what was the best thing to do.

One hot summer day when I was 7 I went to the grocery store with my mom. As we were standing in the checkout line, I turned and looked, and there, staring me in the face, was a rack filled with

Tic-Tacs. After checking to make sure that nobody was looking, I grabbed a box of the sweet orange pills. I figured that I needed something to put in my dry mouth, and because there were plenty there, nobody would miss them. So I put them in my pocket. I was a bit nervous, but I needed something to quench my palate.

About two years later I was sitting in my third-grade classroom. There was a spelling test that day, and I had not studied at all. I thought to myself, *Why study when you can just have the answers right there?* So I wrote all of the words on a sheet of paper, which I placed under my leg right as the teacher passed out the test. Although my heart was racing, getting an A was more important than being honest.

Several years passed, and the cheating continued. My family and I ended up moving to St. Louis, Missouri. I had never lived in the city before, and it was far different from the country life that I was used to. Soon I found myself hanging out with guys who were into smoking, drinking, and stealing. Of course I had no problem keeping up with them. I was a natural. I got so involved with breaking into cars that I started to go out by myself just to steal another radio or radar detector. I knew I had to make money, and stealing was the easiest way. The more I broke into cars, the easier it got. During this time, I also became an atheist (not that I had ever really known God to begin with).

A couple years later I moved to St. Augustine, Florida. I immediately had friends to hang out with, because my cousins lived there. One day as we were driving around, they pulled out a sack of marijuana. Of course I tried it. I started smoking weed every day: before school, during school, and after school. But because I was still cheating in every class, I maintained a decent GPA.

After high school I moved to Orlando to attend a community college. After completing the first year (still creatively maintaining decent grades), I decided one day to go to Jamaica. You see, marijuana had become such a big part of my life that I wanted to learn more about the Rastafarian religion, because Rastafarians smoke marijuana for "spiritual purposes."

I arrived in Jamaica all by myself. I had my backpack, tent, sleeping bag, some clothes, and a few dollars. While there I met a Rasta who said that he would supply me with as much "ganja" as I could sell. I had finally found the key to success: I was going to be rich!

By the time I left Jamaica, I had a couple pounds of this illegal weed in my suitcase. I flew into Miami International Airport, and although I went through customs with drug dogs on me and everything, I didn't get caught. Whew!

About a month later I returned to Jamaica in order to get some more weed to sell. When I returned to the States and again had no problems getting through customs, I knew that there had to be someone, somewhere, watching over me.

Although I was still smoking weed, I started to become more agnostic, believing that there had to be a higher power. One day while on the beach in St. Augustine I cried out, saying, "God, Jah [the name the Rastafarians give for God], Jesus, Tu Kan, Sam, Martian, Lucky Charms, whoever You are, wherever You are, get in touch with me!"

I said that prayer several times over the next couple months. Then my life suddenly started falling apart. I got kicked out of my house and lost my job; my only plan was to return to Jamaica.

A week later my brother Richard, who had already planned a vacation in St. Augustine, drove down from Maryland with his wife, Molly. Molly had been born and raised Adventist, and before they got married, Richard had become an Adventist too. (At the time, I was oblivious to all of this, even though I was the best man in the wedding.)

When they arrived, I began to tell them about my plans to return to Jamaica. My brother, knowing what I had done in the past, didn't think it was such a good idea. As they tried to talk me out of it, I got so upset that I cussed them out more than once. But at the end of their week's stay they invited me to return with them to Maryland to experience their lifestyle.

I sat there dumbfounded, not able to comprehend how, after I had treated them so poorly, they were now inviting me to their house. But something inside me told me that this was the best decision, so I went.

To my unpleasant surprise, "their lifestyle" consisted of working on their newly purchased five-acre farm. I dug ditches, cut trees, trimmed vines. Needless to say, I thought that I had just made one of the biggest mistakes of my life.

Then one morning my brother approached me and asked me if I would like to visit with his pastor. Although I really did not know the man, I was willing to do anything to get off that farm for a few hours.

While in Pastor Rob Vandeman's office, I shared my entire life experience with him. After a couple hours passed he shared some insights and then told me that he wanted to give me a book: *The Message,* by Eugene Peterson. In its covers is found a modern-day translation of the New Testament along with the Psalms and Proverbs. I opened its pages and turned to the first book, Matthew.

But I could not understand what this Jesus guy was trying to teach. Whenever He started teaching a parable, I always picked the wrong outcome. Every night when Richard and Molly returned home, I asked them questions to clarify what I had just read. As they answered, the stories came to life. I began to realize that this Jesus was teaching me things about my own life, even though we had never met.

About a week later I returned to Florida. When my dad picked me up from the airport I told him that I was not completely sure about Jesus and the whole Christianity thing, but that I was going to give Him a shot. The next day I picked up the phone and called a local Adventist church to get directions and times for the upcoming Sabbath service. That following Sabbath I ended up studying the Bible with the pastor for five hours straight. The next weekend the same thing happened. Soon I began to realize that I was no longer using the profanity that I was so accustomed to using, and that God did not create my lungs to inhale smoke, and that I did not need marijuana in order to be a "spiritual person."

Since that time, I have chosen to listen to the Spirit of God every day. The Lord has blessed me beyond my wildest imagination (and it can be wild). I am now a pastor in Washington State.

Looking back, I know there was a small voice speaking to me in the grocery store on that hot summer day. I felt it speaking to me in the classroom while I was cheating. I heard it while I was breaking into cars and while I was trafficking drugs into the country. I have since come to learn that that still, small voice was the Spirit of God convicting me of my sin.

The truth is that we all have a carnal nature inside, and we are born into sin. Sin is a natural desire. However, God tells us that we are the temple of the Holy Spirit (see 1 Corinthians 6:19). We all must come to the place where we choose to either obey the lust of the flesh, the lust of the eyes, the pride of life, . . . or let the Spirit of God abide in us.

1. Have you ever felt convicted that you are doing something wrong?
2. Have you ever thought of where that conviction comes from?
3. How do you feel about sin?
4. What can you do to be free from sin?
5. Can you commit to start listening to the still, small voice inside of you?
6. How will this realization help you in your witness to others?
7. What would you tell someone who was struggling with sin?

Matthew W. Gamble, 26, finds that wherever he is led to lounge is his stompin' grounds. He enjoys reading great books such as Matthew and letters from a guy named Paul. Daily he chooses to listen to the Spirit of God and allow the "old man" to be crucified.

8

THE GREAT CONTROVERSY
Phyllis Scott-Zimmerman

Why Should I Care?

Realizing that God and Satan war over every soul on earth brings suffering and evil into a clear light.

How Can I Know?

Ezekiel 28:11-17	2 Peter 2:4
Isaiah 14:12-15	Jude 6
Colossians 4:3, 4	1 John 3:12
Revelation 12:7-9	1 John 3:8
Matthew 8:29	1 Peter 5:8
Matthew 12:30	Hebrews 1:14
Matthew 6:24	Revelation 20:7-10
John 13:2	Isaiah 14:12
Matthew 4:1-11	Ephesians 6:11-18
Luke 22:31	2 Corinthians 10:3-5
Revelation 12:12	Colossians 2:15
Revelation 12:17	

A little girl stands at the front of a church, mesmerized by the red and gold carpet below. A small wet pool appears below her as her tears drop to the floor. One by one they fall from her eyes as she kneels at the foot of the stage. All around her she hears the voices of her friends as they snicker and elbow one another out of embarrassment. The floor seems hard as the organ plays "Just As I Am," but her heart feels light, knowing she is loved. She has just given her heart to Jesus. Light fills the room; hope takes root in her heart. The future is suddenly bright.

Several years later those same eyes, now embittered and exhausted, fill with tears as the young girl sits in her car and stares out over the city. Blackness surrounds her except for the dancing, flickering lights below. Suffocating in despair as tears flow down her face unnoticed, she no longer fights her feelings.

The girl's old desires and hopes for the future no longer exist. Instead, all around her a morbid presence presses close. She aches from the pain of carrying life's burden. Exhausted and spent, she wants to lay down and never get up. The lyrics of the music she so loves have become her mantra: "Goodbye, cruel world, I am leaving you today. Goodbye, goodbye, goodb—" The words fade into the nothingness, beckoning her to follow. *Tonight,* she resolves, *this miserable existence will end.*

Where had the joy, love, peace, and hope of yesteryears gone? What had happened to her life?

If only she had known. The day she asked the Saviour into her heart she not only received His love and forgiveness; she also gained a mortal enemy bent on destroying her. Although God so loved the world that He *gave,* Satan so hates the world that he *takes.* After the girl accepted Jesus, Satan slowly dismantled her life. Divorce, family violence, alcoholism, and drug abuse lured her away from the Source of life into a lifestyle of destruction.

At first this new life appeared fun. The girl was popular, athletic, and talented. She had close friends, music, drugs, and alcohol conveniently provided for her at little cost (so she thought). Slowly, dabbling with trouble became a way of life: a way to escape the pain of her parents' divorce, a way to cover the anger and rage that brewed inside her. Before she knew it, she was a drug addict and alcoholic. It began to dominate her existence, but she still did not grasp how out of control she had become.

For one entire year in high school the first thing she did every morning was deaden herself with the drug of her choice. She did drugs every evening, hoping to find calm and rest. Gone were all feelings; she had become comfortably numb. And while this numbness swept away her pain and sorrow, it also swept away her will to live.

Night after night the girl stumbled into her room (wallpapered with album covers and posters of her favorite artists), fell into bed with her smoke-filled clothes still on, and waited for the world to stop spinning. Her head pounded from the toxins in her body, and her heart felt overburdened from the emptiness inside. Her mind ached as the voices wrestled inside her head.

"You're no good!" one voice shouted. "No one will ever love you. You have no future."

The other voice spoke in a gentle whisper: "You're not alone. I'm still here."

Confused, yet comforted by the gentle whisper, she would open her old Bible (given to her years ago on the red carpet). In an attempt to find God's love, she would read, "In the beginning God created the heavens and the earth" (Genesis 1:1, NIV), only to black out by the time He made the firmaments. Over and over she would repeat this process, which left her feeling guilty and ashamed.

The girl knew that God existed and that her lifestyle was wrong. She was growing weary of feeling sick, tired, and wasted. She wanted more from life, but she didn't know how to find it. And the more she wanted out, the stronger the forces to keep her in became.

The voice of destruction became so loud that she could no longer hear the gentle whisper. She partied harder and lived life on the edge. Deeper and deeper into emptiness she fell, until night seemed like day and day was still night. All the light was gone. The voices convinced her that she hated life, that she despised herself and it was time to end it all.

✦ ✦ ✦

With one last huge gulp she finishes her bottle of Southern Comfort and turns the key in her car. She grips the steering wheel, tears blinding her momentarily, and shakes her head to clear her vision. She feels her whole body respond to her despair as she plans the last moments of her life. Her lips tremble, and she starts to shake. The engine hums at a hypnotic pitch; it gives her the calm she needs to see her plan through to the end. She wonders out loud, "Who would miss me?"

A familiar voice replies, "No one, and no one loves you. You're alone and will always be alone."

"No one would even mourn my loss," she says as the car lurches toward the cliff.

Suddenly the car stalls just a few feet away from the terrifying plunge. "What?" She furiously turns the key, and the engine begins to roar. The smell of exhaust fills her nostrils as she pumps the gas to keep the car running.

The car begins moving as the exhaust streams out of the tailpipe into the midnight sky.

Gravel crunches under the tires as the edge draws closer. Slowly the girl drives her metal coffin toward her destiny. Inches away now, she anticipates the feeling of weightlessness she will soon feel. Then, at the last minute, darkness envelops her. She feels and hears no more. Unconsciousness saves her from the horror of her own suicide.

Hours later the girl awakes to an intense piercing light and the sounds of birds. "Is this heaven?" she thinks out loud. She wipes her eyes and stares at the leather interior of her car, cluttered with bottles and other paraphernalia. The girl quickly touches her body, wondering where the blood is, why everything is still the same. Slowly she realizes that she passed out before she could kill herself! She drives home, confused and drained.

At home the grandfather clock chimes 3:00 p.m. *Wow! Where did the day go?* she wonders as she tries to lift her pounding head off the sofa. Slipping on her sandals, she makes her way to the mailbox outside. "Bill, bill, junk, junk," she mumbles under stale breath. Then something catches her eye: a colorful brochure emblazoned on the front with a picture of a provocatively made-up woman drinking from a golden goblet, the number 666 on her forehead. The girl reads on, and as the brochure unfolds, so does her curiosity. The word "FREE!" entices her to call and see what this is all about.

The girl makes reservations for the Revelation Seminar, and several days later she and her two cohorts enter a small white church. Two gray-haired, conservative-looking women greet them.

"Uh, do you have reservations?" one woman finally speaks rather timidly.

"Yup. Where do we sit?" the girl says loudly. Not even waiting for the women to reply, she walks up to the front row. The young pastor looks rather intimidated, but continues to speak.

Hung over, tired, and high, she sits and tries to absorb the material he presents. The benches are hard, but the temperature is just right for sleeping. Yet something about the white walls, the green carpet, and the words of the young pastor continue to intrigue her. After the first meeting she decides not to get high for the next one.

Three months later she was baptized into the Seventh-day Adventist Church. Gone was the voice that shouted her self-worthlessness. Gone was the desire to self-destruct. Gone was her appetite for drugs and alcohol. All these things were replaced with the sweet and tender love of Jesus. Her longing to serve Him was immense.

The turning point in the girl's life came when she learned the truth about the Saviour's love and the devil's hatred. She learned that there is a battle raging and that every human soul is involved. No person can stand in neutrality: Each has chosen a side, consciously or not. The girl realized that the voices she heard through the drugs she had ingested were the attempts of her spiritual enemy to destroy her. The devil, her adversary, had worked fast and furiously to take her life before the seminar. She learned that Satan had been studying human nature for thousands of years and knew something was brewing. He knew that his enemy, the Holy Spirit, was about to reach her heart.

The girl's journey to the cross was not easy—the adversary made sure of that. Old drug friends came out of the woodwork, opportunities for free drugs were everywhere, and a violent car accident weeks before her baptism proved that the devil wanted to keep her in his camp. However, on the day of her baptism the devil lost. He lost the battle for her soul and gained another enemy in the battle for humanity.

Because the devil knows he will eventually lose the war, he is filled with fury and intent on bringing down as many humans as he can with him. He will not give up. Even when Jesus splits the sky and takes His people home, Satan will continue his deception until the last deceived soul is burned and he himself is annihilated in the lake of fire.

Yes, the great controversy is real to me, for the story above is my own. Back and forth the battle for my soul raged on. Satan had enticed me with the empty promise of popularity, love, and acceptance through the world of drugs. Satan wanted me to believe that all my drugs were given to me free. However, I learned that nothing Satan has to offer is free. It will eventually cost your soul.

Just look around. Look at all the violence, hate, poverty, and disease. Look into your own life and see the struggles and temptation that have come your way. The great controversy is not something that happened a long time ago. No, it is happening here and now in the hearts of us all.

When I served Satan, I was a great benefit to his kingdom, leading many people astray and into a life of destruction. Although he used me, he still hated me and was ultimately set to destroy my body and my soul.

We are reminded that the weapons of our warfare are not of this world, that we battle not against flesh and blood but against spiritual beings that we cannot see. The battle line for allegiance was drawn long before time began; it is up to you to decide which side to fight on and how effective a warrior you will be. At the end of my life I want to be able to say, "I have fought the good fight" (2 Timothy 4:7, NIV). I long to look up into the eyes of my Commander and Lord and hear Him say: "'Well done, good and faithful servant' (Matthew 25:21, NIV). Put down your sword and enter into the kingdom prepared for you."

1. How do you know that the great controversy is real?

2. How do you know that the devil is real?

3. What can you do to shield yourself in this battle?

4. How would you answer the frequently asked question: Why did God not just destroy Satan in the beginning?

5. In what ways have you seen the intensity of the devil increase in your lifetime?

6. How does it make you feel to know that there is an enemy out there who hates you as much as God loves you?

7. Which of the following describes your current spiritual condition? (Explain)
A. Solider of Christ
B. Fence walker
C. Enemy of the state

8. What does the Bible mean when it talks about the difficulty of serving two masters (see Matthew 6:24)?

9. What role did the crucifixion of Christ play in the great controversy?

10. How was the great controversy exposed in the desert (see Matthew 4:1-11)?

Phyllis Scott-Zimmerman, 32, lives in Berrien Springs, Michigan, with her husband, DaRon, and son, Anthony. She teaches physical education classes and is a self-defense advocate and instructor. She enjoys cycling, weight training, and gardening.

THE LIFE, DEATH, AND RESURRECTION OF CHRIST

Braden Pewitt

Why Should I Care?
Believing that Jesus lived, died, and rose again with me in mind reminds me how much He loves me now.

How Can I Know?

John 3:16, 17

Romans 3:22, 23

Romans 3:25, 26

Romans 5:6-9

Romans 5:9-11

Romans 6:23

Romans 8:1

Luke 19:10

Titus 3:3-8

Hebrews 2:9

1 John 5:11, 12

Ephesians 5:25-27

1 Timothy 1:15

Isaiah 53:4-6

2 Timothy 1:8-10

2 Corinthians 5:17-19

Romans 8:35-39

Ephesians 5:1, 2

Revelation 5:9, 10

1 Corinthians 15:21, 22

2 Corinthians 5:21

Colossians 1:21, 22

John 15:12-14

The crimson capes of the Roman soldiers caught my attention. Their glistening spears, sturdy helmets, and powerful breastplates filled me with awe. *How cool,* I thought. *I'd love to dress like that for a day.* So I signed my name on the list in the guys' dorm lobby and hoped I'd get a part in the Sonrise pageant.

Every Easter at Southern Adventist University the college church produces a walk-through drama of the life of Christ. Hundreds of community people come to relive those scenes. Familiar sidewalks become loud marketplaces. The sounds of sheep, goats, and chickens fill the air around the library. The grass outside the guys' dorm soaks up the tears of a dying, struggling Jesus as He resists the devil's urges to give up the idea of saving humanity. The shadows lurk with cruel soldiers waiting to torture the Son of God to death.

I got the part, the day finally came for dress rehearsal, and the wardrobe crew handed me my uniform. I knew I was going to enjoy being a Roman. I stood in my dorm room that night admiring the bulky, handsome soldier staring back at me in the mirror. I spun to watch the cape billow behind me, and I thrust my spear in front of me with enough force to run through any impostor. I was certain I made a magnificent warrior.

The morning of Sonrise, my girlfriend, Joie, helped me lace up my sandals. I then impressed her with the same swift moves. She agreed that I made a stunning Roman soldier, but she had to leave quickly to meet up with the other Jewish mobsters in the scene at Pilate's hall. I headed toward the Crucifixion scene to find out my position for the day, excited to meet up with my comrades at the cross. It would be our job to "crucify" Jesus without hurting the actor beneath the white costume. The scene director gave me the responsibility of placing crimson liquid soap on the hands and feet of Jesus to appear as blood to the onlookers. The other soldiers would cover my actions from sight by holding the body in place. Another soldier would slam the edge of the cross with the sledgehammer to portray graphically the act of driving the nails into the feet and hands of Jesus. We were all amazed at how real the scene would look to the crowd.

We practiced heaving the cross into place. I was shocked at how much it weighed and how roughly it dropped into the hole prepared for it. We had to try several times before we got it up smoothly without tipping or dropping it. With a half hour to go before the first group came through, we were prepared to do our job well.

Before the day was through, nine groups of people would come to our scene in half-hour increments. Each crowd would follow the cross dragged by Simon. Soldiers from Pilate's hall would turn over the tortured Jesus to us, and we would do our job. In one day we would publicly crucify Jesus nine times.

At 9:30 we heard the first crowd approaching. We knew by the size that there were several hundred people in the group. I stood tall on Golgotha hill with my cruelest expression, waiting to bloody up the man called Jesus. I proudly turned to let the air catch my cape and billow it out behind me. That first scene went smoothly, and we had enough time before the next one to congratulate ourselves on how well we'd portrayed the Crucifixion.

The second and third came and went, but I began to notice a change in myself. I was really getting into the part, and it was hard to snap out between scenes. With hatred I would shove the actor in white onto the cross. I felt strange treating someone so calm with such cruelty. And then there was the sticky soap: It was hard to get off my hands. After they'd taken the body off the cross I'd kneel in the grass below and try in vain to wipe it off. Though tough on the outside, my heart began to bleed on the inside. Each time I looked up into the tortured face of the man I'd put there, I hurt deeper.

After the fifth or sixth crucifixion, I turned away as the crowd slowly moved toward the gym and the Resurrection scene. The soft music playing through the speakers only tore at my heart more. Tears stung my eyes, but I couldn't cry. I was a Roman soldier, and my cape still billowed behind me. I must push on for the last few scenes. So with even more rage I shoved the man in white toward the cross and ripped his garments off him. I crushed him onto the rough, rugged cross and watched the crimson blood drip down his body. I helped drop the cross in place and mock him as he died. But I couldn't escape my horror. Why would God let us treat Him like this? Why did He have to die like this?

With these questions plaguing my mind I tried again to stay in character. Again the crowd silently left the cross, following the body of Christ. The soft music was playing, and I could hear sniffles among the onlookers. We had indeed preformed our job well.

But was it too well? As I looked sternly into the crowd, the eyes of a child came into focus before me. He was a tiny boy riding on his father's shoulders. Tears brimmed his eyes as he looked toward me. The father stopped in front of me and those tiny eyes above him stared at me in wonder and dread. Then the boy spoke in a trembling voice.

"You didn't really kill Jesus, did you?"

I stood in silence, stunned by his words. What could I say? Yet my silence only crushed the lad more. Finally they turned and merged into the crowd. But the boy left me trying to escape the reality he had placed on me. I hadn't done anything wrong, had I? I was only playing a part. Inside I screamed, *It wasn't me, kid. I didn't kill Jesus. I didn't do it!* But the words froze within me as I turned to leave. For there . . . there on my hands was His blood.

I cried there beneath His cross, for I knew with surety then that I had killed Jesus. It was me. The boy was right. Yet it was all so much more real than costumes and red soap. Jesus had really died. He had really bled. And it was because of my sins that He'd died. God once said that if anyone sinned, they must die. I knew I had sinned many times . . . but death? I looked at my bloody hands again. I was scared to realize that this blood was the result of my sin.

But this blood on my hands was not mine. It belonged to the Son of God. Why? Because God was willing to experience His own punishment for me and die to pay the price.

The wind blew my cape out behind me again as I knelt at the cross. But this time I grabbed it and held it close. Then I stood up and looked into the great blue sky and spoke out loud to the risen Saviour. A smile spread across my face. *I knew He was alive.*

"Thank You!" I prayed. "Thank You for saving me!"

1. Why couldn't God just pardon our sins instead of coming to die on the cross Himself?

2. What does Jesus' death on the cross tell you about the kind of love your God has for you?

3. How can understanding the enormity of God's sacrifice for you change your everyday life?

4. What would you tell someone who is trying to get to heaven by being good?

5. Are you willing to accept what Jesus did on the cross as the full payment for your sin?

6. How can you help those around you realize what Jesus did for them?

7. Why were Jesus' life and death necessary to bridge the gulf between Himself and us?

Braden Pewitt, 24, is currently a missionary in training with Adventist Frontier Missions. He plans to be in Cambodia soon with his beautiful wife, Joie, planting a church among a group of people who have never heard about Jesus before.

10

THE EXPERIENCE OF SALVATION

Sarah Hager Schroetlin

Why Should I Care?

Feeling the weight of my sin, and realizing that sin separates me from God, leads me to confess my need and accept the salvation that God offers through the death of His Son.

How Can I Know?

Psalm 51:1, 3, 10	Romans 8:15-17
Proverbs 28:13	2 Peter 1:4
John 12:32	Romans 3:10
Romans 5:6-10	Isaiah 64:6
Titus 3:5	Isaiah 59:1
James 2:22	1 John 1:9
2 Corinthians 5:21	Romans 3:23
Zechariah 3:2	

I sat on my metal chair in the primary Sabbath school room. The hardness and coldness of it didn't even creep into my consciousness. My eyes were glued on my teacher, Shirley. She spoke quietly, her small hands fluttering in vivid description. You would have thought, from the unusual stillness of the small bodies before her, that it was the mission story she was telling, complete with horrible diseases rotting away the limbs of human beings and head-hunters-turned-vegetarian just at the last crucial moment.

But that wasn't it. Shirley was describing how God had saved her. She was very entertaining no matter what story she told. Shirley could probably have described some law of physics and had us in stitches with the humor of it. Here and there she threw in something that made us giggle. Her sins were sometimes funny. But as she wove for us the tale of her salvation, I began to catch a glimpse of the "lost" feeling Shirley had endured during a childhood of abuse, an early marriage to a dangerous man, years of poverty and depression and bad decisions and sometimes no choices at all.

Alternately my heart fell like a heavy rock at my feet, then soared with hope. She didn't make her language *small* to match our smallness. Just as in Zechariah's vision about standing before God in filthy rags, Shirley had been lost in sin—dark and horrible. God said to Satan, "Is this not a brand plucked from the fire?" (Zechariah 3:2, NKJV). God came and rescued Shirley like that, saving her in all of her confusion. He gave her a new life.

Lined up in a row, wearing our shining Sabbath faces and fancy Sabbath clothes, we somehow grasped that what Shirley had found, we needed. Her story was something so true and real that I was looking out of wet and blurry eyes as I listened. I ached to have a salvation experience such as hers. I always read my Sabbath school lesson. I memorized my memory verses. I enjoyed going to church. Still, I felt gypped. I wanted a story to tell, but had not experienced anything distressing enough to warrant a heavenly rescue, except maybe a visit to the dentist, something I loathed more than anything else in life. And so far God had never delivered me from that.

So began a journey that lasted for several years. I wanted to be saved and go to heaven when Jesus came back. But so far as I could tell, I was as saved as I could get. Why couldn't it have been more exciting? Why couldn't I have been rescued like Shirley was? At that time in my life I shared the experience of many evangelical Christian young people. I grew up in the faith. I knew "the truth" and wasn't surprised by any new sermon. The stories were old companions. I was entrenched in my denomination's way of life. I wavered on the brink of the dark abyss: I was doing everything I knew to live a good life, but I knew that we are saved "not by works of righteousness which we have done, but according to His mercy He saved us" (Titus 3:5, NKJV). So how was I to know if I truly was saved? I didn't feel as though I had a life-changing experience to which I could trace my trail of faith.

Jump forward a year or two. I crept down the stairs of my home in the early dawn. With my forehead resting on the cool bars I peered at my mother's back. Wrapped in a blanket, she sat hunched over at her little desk in the corner. She was so busy. All day she cleaned up after and cooked for four children and a husband. She made lunches and made us practice piano and drove us around. At night she nursed a baby and rocked and got us water. Yet here she sat, awake so early. She read a Bible text, underlined it with her red pencil, then wrote it in her little notebook. Then read another one. She cried a lot as she did this. I could see her back quivering . . . hear her sobs as she learned that Jesus really loved her and forgave her. I watched in silence as my own mother accepted God's salvation for her torn-up heart. God's "exceedingly great and precious promises" were giving Mama life, and she was becoming a partaker "of the divine nature, having escaped the corruption that is in the world" (2 Peter 1:4, NKJV).

I turned and tiptoed back up the stairs. Where did her tears come from? What a fountain of sorrow had been locked up inside of her and was now being released! She had found something that I wanted very badly for myself. A personal, saving, refreshing experience with God.

My salvation story finally came. God had been working it out all along. I was headstrong and willful. I struggled with pride and independence, and anger got in the way of my peace. Finally God convicted me of the seriousness of the sins that were a part of my nature. I began to see things in myself *every day* that made me not like myself very much. I experienced sorrow and guilt about the distance I was putting between myself and God. This was a heavy burden for an insecure teen to carry around on her shoulders. I began reading the Bible not for the stories, but for the "exceedingly great and precious promises" I found there. I was hungry for peace. I needed to know my worth in God's eyes. "He who covers his sins will not prosper, but whoever confesses and forsakes them will have mercy" (Proverbs 28:13, NKJV). I fell on that mercy. I just crashed right where I was and fell.

Once I finally broke under that burden, the fall really wasn't that far, and the landing was a soft one: right into the lap of the Saviour. My hot tears flowed as I took to heart the fact that "God demonstrates His own love toward us, in that while we were still sinners, Christ died for us" (Romans 5:8, NKJV). I had finally experienced my own "salvation story."

I have told three salvation stories here. So what does salvation look like? What is the process of the experience of salvation? I think it is just this: God allows us to feel the weight of separation from Him. Our horrible physical or mental or spiritual anguish seems inescapable. Then He steps in and rescues us. The amazing gift of His dying Son proves His love, and it is this very goodness of God that leads us to repent (see Romans 2:4). God is good to me every day. My rescue is an ongoing, daily gift in which I rejoice. So I can sit on a cold, metal chair and listen to stories of salvation, or peer through the banisters of life and actually watch salvation occurring in another life, and I can cry out: "He is so good! He has done this very thing for me! Praise God! I am saved!"

1. Do you feel "saved"?
2. Can you *be* saved without *feeling* saved?
3. Have you experienced release from sin in a specific way?
4. How can you repent if you don't feel sorry or don't know what you have done to *need* repentance?
5. What is your experience of salvation?
6. Have you shared it with someone lately?
7. Do you know someone who may be encouraged by listening to your rescue story?
8. Has your heart been warmed and humbled by the awesomeness of Christ's death?

Sarah Hager Schroetlin, 26, lives in Farmington, Washington, with her husband, Dennis, and new baby boy, Avery. She enjoys her home and family and a rare full night of sleep. She is amazed at what she is learning about God by being a wife and mother.

11

THE CHURCH

Sara Grable

Why Should I Care?

As the church, we are the body of Christ, called to work together as His family.

How Can I Know?

Genesis 12:3	Colossians 1:17, 18
Ephesians 4:11-16	Acts 20:25-28
Ephesians 3:8-11	Colossians 3:12-17
Matthew 28:19, 20	Galatians 6:9, 10
Matthew 16:13-20	John 4:23, 24
Ephesians 2:19-22	1 Corinthians 14:26
Ephesians 1:22, 23	Ephesians 4:3-6
Ephesians 5:23-30	1 Peter 4:4-12

Heat pressed me into the road and drew sheets of sweat from my body. I watched the powder-soft sand sift through my sandals and mix with my sweat, forming small brown rivers. I sighed. I'd taken this walk five times already this week, and the familiarity of the sewer canal bobbing with bottles and trash, the nearby row of greasy fried chicken shops, and the insolent stares of passing banana vendors depressed me. Back to school again.

So far my year as a student missionary in Belize City, Belize, had seemed perfectly typical: uncomfortable beginnings with nervous, giggling students and strange things wiggling in my rice, the adjustments of culture shock and teaching responsibility, and—finally—comfort and productivity in my new environment. The more open I became, the more my students responded. The more I got to know the people around me, the more I fit in.

Church was different, though. Somehow it tossed me right back into the same problems of discomfort and insecurity I thought I'd conquered in the first month or two. Church was strange. Instead of driving to an air-conditioned sanctuary with gilt-edged Bible prints and muted pastel carpets, I repeated my daily trek to the school where I taught. Church was in my classroom. Brightly chalked greetings graced the faded chalkboard, and my desk sat robed in pink satin splendor. Otherwise, nothing had changed.

I dragged my feet more slowly every Sabbath, more and more anxious to avoid the tiny classroom, its stifling heat, and hymns pitched so high I couldn't sing them. I disliked the beaming Mr. Rosales, moustache freshly greased and twirled, and his friendly bobbing as I entered. I disliked squeezing myself into the desks I addressed daily, disliked the fervent, weekly sermons on the value of evangelism.

What bothered me the most, though, was the feeling that I didn't belong. Why didn't anyone talk to me? Why didn't anyone ask me home for dinner? During the synchronized ups and downs of prayers, hymns, and responses, I watched the people around me. A few tiny grannies fanned themselves with folded paper fans. The men all seemed middle-aged, impressive in their three-piece suits. The women sat silent through the service, grouping afterward to discuss children and food, things I had no useful opinions on.

One day after church I lay on my bed, exhausted and disgruntled again. I twisted out from under my sheet and wiped the sweat from behind my knees. With an offended air I repeated the familiar litany of offenses, of differences, of negatives. No one talked to me, no one noticed me, no one cared if I came. I could handle a strange place and new ways of thinking when I was teaching and in charge, but at church nobody even tried to do things my way.

I shifted again and closed my eyes, lovingly polishing memories about the perfections of my previous churches. I remembered classes with people my age, where we discussed things instead of reading straight from the quarterly. I remembered pews and pianos and flowers up front. I remembered potlucks: Mom's famous casseroles, salads with real lettuce, and the mandatory lime Jell-O with pears and silver sprinkles that I could steal off its top.

This day, though, a new memory began to nuzzle at the edge of my brain. I remembered my baptism nearly 10 years earlier at Lost Lake camp meeting in Washington state—how the icy lake water had pricked my legs as I waded out waist-deep with my friend Jenny. Instead of a baptismal robe, I wore an oversized T-shirt; its pink and white stripes billowed around my legs and dragged as I walked. As I listened to the pastor, my throat shrunk and breath came more quickly. I was nervous, excited, overwhelmed with love. Next came a sharp intake of breath as I dipped beneath the water and a grin that wouldn't stop as I emerged. What I remembered most, though, as I lay wishing for the coolness of the lake once more, was the row of smiling faces that had lined the lake's edge: their off-key singing, their hugs as I emerged. I remembered Grandma Loretta and her proud smile. I remembered Mike Cassano and the small devotional that he tucked into my hands with a special note inside. I remembered the people.

Smiling at the happy memories, I slipped my feet into sandals and shuffled from my room to the kitchen to hunt up some tortillas left over from lunch, stopping briefly to make sure no lime Jell-O was hiding in the back of the fridge. Tortillas in hand, I returned to my room, thoughts now intent on letter writing and a phone call home.

So it ends up that I don't know exactly how or when it happened. Maybe I gave up. Maybe, just a little, I grew up. But still, there was a change. Instead of strangers, I found myself going to church to be with family, my family. In my new home and my new church I found friends—not to replace the old, but to join them.

Public speaking has always made me sweat, but my knees have never wobbled quite as much as they did when I stood in front of my 23-member church for the first time to read the mission story.

My English major tongue garbled *and's* and *the's,* and my hands couldn't stop poking hair behind my ear and pushing up my glasses. It wasn't the speaking part that was hard; it was the feeling that with this story—about some jungle missionary? a successful investment project?—I was admitting that I'd been wrong. I was saying "Sorry."

I'd felt superior. I'd felt as though I didn't belong.

I had been wrong.

The last few weeks I spent with my church were amazing. The louder I sang the less I minded the monotones behind me. The more hands I shook, the less I felt a stranger. And suddenly I was involved. I gave prayer and read stories, but what mattered was that I *knew* the people I prayed for and read to.

On my last Sabbath at church the theme was celebrating mothers. There were special plastic roses for each grandma, each mom, even one for the young woman expecting a baby. And there was a flower for me—no reason, just love for a church member who finally belonged.

I like the body metaphor. If a church is going to live, its separate parts have to work together, have to listen to each other. Unfortunately, I spent most of my year in Belize as a disgruntled appendage—a misplaced appendix, maybe, or a reluctant tonsil. Maybe I was toe jam—something useless.

By the end of my stay, though, I was content. Probably still toe jam—but cheerful toe jam. I came to see the grace of the people who would let me be a part of their church body, even welcome me, after my long months of angry silence and absence.

When I stepped off the plane in America, I was bombarded by the objects and things I had missed: hot showers, fast food, air-conditioning, supermarkets. Even better, I spent time with my family and friends, with the people I loved. Somehow, though, the reunion wasn't quite as complete as I'd planned it would be. I was glad to be home. Of course. I'd spent many lonely nights wishing for just that. In the back of my mind, though, was a bit of restlessness.

There still is. That's because, in my moments of truth, I wish for the bit of body that taught me to feel the pulse of love from the heart of God that holds us still together, always complete.

1. What types of things often make it difficult to work together as a church body?
2. What can we learn from the biblical church about the way we should relate to one another?
3. How is it possible for separate individuals to become "one in Christ"?
4. What common things can hold us together as a church?
5. What is the purpose of the church body? What should be its goals?
6. How can you work to strengthen the church body?
7. What is Christ's role as the head of the church?

Sara Grable, 22, spent one year in Belize, Central America, as a freshman English teacher. She is now a whiz at freshman grammar. Her compulsive habits include traveling to new and jungly places, writing poetry, perfecting the art of Thai cooking, and spending time with a very significant other.

12

THE REMNANT AND ITS MISSION

Shane Anderson

Why Should I Care?

Understanding the remnant and its mission frees me from Satan's deceptions so that I may know Jesus better.

How Can I Know?

John 17:3	Revelation 14:6-12
John 14:6	John 3:16
Daniel 1-9	Romans 3:23, 24
Revelation 12 (particularly verse 17)	Romans 6:23
Revelation 19:10	Ephesians 2:8, 9
Revelation 13 (particularly verse 14)	John 14:15
2 Thessalonians 2:8-10	1 John 2:1-6
I Timothy 4:1	James 1:22-25 (particularly 25)
Matthew 24:23-27	John 8:31, 32
Matthew 28:19, 20	Revelation 21:1-4
Acts 1:8	Revelation 22:12-14
John 10:10	

That does it! I thought to myself. *I can't take this anymore.* And with that, my hand shot up like a viper striking its prey. I had a question for the professor, and I was *going to be heard,* ready or not.

The incident that caused all this commotion occurred when I was a sophomore theology major at Walla Walla College. I was sitting in Research Writing in Religion, a class in which fledgling theologians like myself were taught the basics of using sources for sermon preparation and related tasks. While religious research can cover a wide range of topics, our class at that time dealt with only one for the entire quarter: the second coming of Christ.

Now, you would think that for a major in theology at a Seventh-day Adventist institution, doing papers and hearing lectures on the second coming of Christ would be a desirable thing. After all, I'd probably need to reference Christ's return a time or two after graduation when I became a pastor, and this class would be just the thing to prime the pump. Or so I thought.

Indeed, the class went fine for many weeks—until that day when my instructor produced from his folder The Thing. To some it was only a piece of paper. But to me, The Thing was a vile instrument of apocalyptic propaganda used by the church's evangelistic machine to lure the innocent to destruction.

The Thing . . . was a Revelation Seminar brochure.

It was a fine example of the breed, too: the beasts, the dragon, the prostitute, guns, blood, wine in expensive goblets, the whole nine yards in all their tricolor, quad-folded glory. And it was their unveiling that made my hand shoot up to spew forth my objections.

When at last called upon, I made my objections clear to the class. "What right to do we have," I sputtered, "to scare people into the church with those beasts? And what right do we have to say that Jesus is coming soon when we've been saying that for 150 years? And how can we be so bold—so arrogant—as to say that we and we alone are the remnant church of Bible prophecy?"

There followed a somewhat lengthy pause, but at last the professor gave his reply. I have no doubt it was a good one, for he was a staunch believer in our church and its mission in the world. But I confess that I heard none of it. I was not in a listening mood.

✦ ✦ ✦

Just a guess, but I'll bet that many of you have felt that way about

Adventism (or your church) before too. Maybe you feel that way now. After all, Adventism has been many things, but never a fence-sitting religion. Adventism has instead specialized in drawing clear lines in the sand, in calling people to a decision either for or against its understanding of God. "Gray" is not one of our primary colors.

And unfortunately, there are thousands of young adults just like me in that research class who see only the "beastly brochure" interpretation of the remnant and its mission, take it for gospel, and never bother to formulate their own interpretation.

You and I do not need someone else to tell us about the remnant and its mission (though I relish every opportunity to hear such renditions—they help me process my own thoughts). What we need instead is an opportunity to discover these things for ourselves. It is an opportunity that will cost you dearly (nothing worth dying for comes cheaply). But let me gently challenge you to pay the price, however high . . . or else consider another place to worship.

How dare you say that! you might be thinking. I dare say it because someone once cared enough to say it to me a year after I started pastoring my first church. And as a result, I met Jesus for the first time.

The incident happened after yet another Sabbath when I had preached what I considered to be a pretty good sermon. It was not an "Adventist" sermon, though a preacher who believed in the remnant and its mission could have easily brought out an Adventist perspective. But my thoughts on the church had changed little since that day in Research Writing in Religion. I was a closet non-Adventist on my own secret mission to bring "grace" to a denomination that I saw as hopelessly legalistic (never mind that I hadn't experienced grace yet myself, let alone a close relationship with Christ). My sermon that Sabbath was a clear reflection of this mission.

An elderly gentleman in whom I had confided some of my disagreements with the church talked with me on the phone following the service that week. He asked me three questions that were to change my life forever:

"Shane, when you stand up on Sabbath morning to preach, isn't it assumed by all the members in attendance that you believe what the Adventist Church believes?"

H'mmm, I thought. "Well, yeah, I guess so."

"So if you don't believe what the Adventist Church believes, yet you continue in the pulpit Sabbath after Sabbath, doesn't that make you a hypocrite?"

I started to sweat a little. "Yes, I suppose . . . it does," I responded, wondering where all this was going.

"Then don't you think that *for the sake of your own integrity,* you had better decide whether or not you believe what Adventism believes or else find another denomination to preach in?"

After a long pause I responded the only way I honestly could. "Yes."

Unbelievable! For years I had pointed to Seventh-day Adventists, their church administrators, and their apparently bait-and-switch evangelistic tactics and cried, "Hypocrites!" But now, shock of shocks, their shoe was on my foot—I was the only hypocrite visible at that moment. And for the first time in my life, someone had had the care and the courage to point out that *for the sake of my own integrity*—not because the church would kick me out—I needed either to agree with Adventism or to move on to a church that I *could* agree with.

I had never seen things that way before. But it was reality nonetheless. And I decided to find out whether the Adventist teaching about the remnant and its mission was heaven-sent or hoax.

For two weeks I quit the ministry. I did no preaching, visiting, Bible studies, or phone calling. I read, studied, and prayed for at least eight hours a day, seven days a week. I read everything I could get my hands on concerning the remnant and its mission, utilizing both Adventist and non-Adventist sources. Of course, my primary study was in the Bible itself. And at the end of those two weeks I came to a conclusion: It was all true.

The beasts, the time lines, the prophecies, the concept of an end-time remnant, the Sabbath, etc., etc.—it was all true. Not that I was happy about this. In fact, I was probably one of the more reluctant believers in the technical side of Adventism that the church had ever seen. But I could prove these things from the Bible (without Ellen White), and thus could only conclude that they were true.

And then, just after the end of those two weeks, came the best discovery of all. I discovered Christ and His grace. I learned that sal-vation was indeed free, that in fact *I* had been the legalist all those years, that Jesus loved me whether I followed Him or not. I was lib-erated, set free. I was for *the very first time* a Seventh-day Adventist, a true member of the remnant and a believer in its mission.

And what is that remnant and its mission?

My two weeks of study helped me understand that the concept of a remnant people—a final group in love with Jesus at the end of time who share the gospel with the world—is biblical. But it also showed me that the idea of a remnant *denomination* is not. The Adventist Church is therefore *not* the remnant denomination of Bible prophecy, simply because no such thing is mentioned in Scripture.

Instead, the remnant described in Revelation 12:17 and else-where is a magnetic movement (note the emphasis on action) *by* and *for* Christ, one that is called to attract others to Him. So we are not *the* remnant church (which surely smacks of arrogance and elitism). We are instead the church called to *gather* the remnant. In other words, we who are Adventists are not all there is; there are millions more to come! The focus is on service, *not* exclusivity, and thus an arrogant Adventist is no Adventist at all.

And what is the mission of this remnant? *To make fully devoted followers of Christ who help others withstand Satan's final deceptions.* (This is the three angels' messages in condensed form.) My two weeks of study reminded me that Satan has always tried to deceive people. But at the end of time he knows that the jig is almost up. It is then that he plays his best cards, hoping to take as many people down with him as possible when Christ returns. Spiritualism, pa-ganism, a degradation of the Sabbath, and other deceptions are all major players in the end-time game.

This being the case, one of the best lessons learned during my two weeks of study was this: *the only reason* Adventist doctrines speak of Satan's deceptions is to remove them *and enable a full re-lationship with Jesus.* Doctrines are not ends in themselves, nor the reason we exist. Knowing, for instance, that when you're dead, you're dead (belief 25) seemed useless to me—until I saw that it would set free my next-door neighbor who up till now has been listening to his dearly departed "wife" say Christianity is a hoax. And keeping the Sabbath holy seemed like small potatoes—until I learned that the Sabbath, a symbol of righteousness by faith and not works (see Exodus 31:12, 13; Deuteronomy 5:15; Ezekial 12:12, 20), can free millions from legalism. And on and on it goes. In fact, no doctrine of the Adventist Church is a stand-alone doctrine, but a doorway into deeper friendship with Christ. If someone tells you otherwise, they don't know the doctrine.

That's why after those weeks of studying about Adventist doctrine, I soon ran smack into the arms of Jesus. And I don't plan on leaving anytime soon.

Sitting in that research class in college, I could not have imagined the life I live with Jesus today in the Adventist Church. I will live for Him and die for Him here; I have found my church home. I will give my life to seeing that the end-time deceptions of Satan are obliterated for as many people as possible. Not that they may know the truth, but that they may know the One who is truth.

The elderly gentleman who challenged me to know what I stood for passed away last year. But his call continues, and I place it before you today: Find out what you believe. Let nothing stand in your way. And if you see fit, come and join me in setting people free to find fulfillment in Jesus, His remnant, and its mission.

1. Do you know Christ? Has Adventism helped you know Christ better or worse? How so?

2. How might you explain Adventism from the Bible in a way that it is truly Christ-centered?

3. "Good works do not define the remnant; they simply reveal it." Agree or disagree? Can you give biblical support for your answer?

4. Why do Adventists get accused of being legalists for keeping the Saturday Sabbath? From the Bible, how might you show a Christian of another faith that this isn't true?

5. Of the following, which of Satan's deceptions do you think are the greatest threat to a relationship with Christ?:
   ✦ Evolution
   ✦ "A little sin is OK"

- ✦ Eternally burning hell
- ✦ Salvation by works
- ✦ "There is no law of God in effect today"
- ✦ Spiritualism/immortality of the soul
- ✦ (Pick your own)

6. Do you have friends who are currently involved in one of the deceptions in question 5? How might you help them? (What would Jesus do?)

7. Is the picture of God in Adventism worth dying for? Why or why not? If not, what would need to be changed in order to make it worth dying for?

8. Do you need to study your Bible more to discover what you believe? If so, how might you start?

Shane Anderson, 29, lives in Everett, Washington, with his stellar wife, Darlene, and brand-new beautiful baby girl, Sierra. He loves a good game of basketball, amateur auto racing, and mountain biking. His consuming passion is to see people sell out to the Gospel of Christ found in the three angels' messages of Revelation 14, with a passion for church planting being a close second. He and his Research Writing in Religion professor (Alden Thompson) are still good friends, even after Shane's spouting off in class.

13

UNITY IN THE BODY OF CHRIST

Abbie Hilton

Why Should I Care?

Unity is one of the identifying features of the followers of Christ, and without it, effective soul-winning is difficult or impossible.

How Can I Know?

Psalm 133:1

John 13:34, 35

John 15:1-6

John 17:10, 11

John 17:20-23

1 Corinthians 1:10

1 Corinthians 12:4-6

1 Corinthians 12:12, 13

2 Corinthians 13:11

Galatians 3:26-29

Ephesians 4:3-6

Ephesians 4:11-16

1 John 3:2, 3

Romans 6:3-6

Romans 15:5, 6

James 2:9

When I decided two years ago to be a missionary in Taiwan, I had vague visions of living in a Japanese-style house with paper walls and bead curtains. My fuzzy mental image included a motherly missionary woman or housekeeper who would direct Bible study in the evenings while I and a dozen other devout missionaries sat on mats and ate noodles and rice with chopsticks.

Well, I got the chopsticks right. Thankfully, a little research on Taiwan dispelled many of my misconceptions long before I got on the plane. I traded my paper houses for apartments made of concrete, tile, and plaster. The food was far more delicious and fantastic than I could have envisioned, and the "motherly" mentor turned out to be my Chinese registrar, a woman perhaps 10 years my senior who was supposed to teach me how to function in a semimodern country where both the written and spoken language are incomprehensible to a foreigner.

The culture was an adjustment. However, I had braced myself for enormous change, and none of it really shocked me. Until I met the other missionaries.

There were nine Adventist Bible/English schools in Taiwan when I came, and the school to which I was assigned was the newest, requiring only three teachers. Aaron had been there two months when I arrived, and we were already casually acquainted. Derek flew in about a week later. He was from California, and I was a bit leery. I'd heard about those California Christians . . .

Derek confirmed my suspicions on our first day at work. Aaron and I were talking about books, and he said, "Actually, I think most reading is a waste of time."

The literature lover in me recoiled in horror. *Truly,* I thought, *I am in the land of the enemy! How can I get along with someone who hates books?*

But if our hobbies had been our only divisions, we would have had little to overcome. I quickly discovered that the most difficult of our beliefs, at least in the mission field, would not be any of the typical doctrines of our religion. In actual practice the hardest of our beliefs would be unity.

The majority of returning student missionaries can attest that interpersonal conflict is the primary problem in most missions. This is distressing, since Christ said, "By this all men will know that you are my disciples, if you love one another" (John 13:35, NIV). Jesus was deeply concerned that His followers be united in purpose and love. John records the last prayer of Jesus before His crucifixion as a prayer for His disciples. "Holy Father," said Jesus, "protect them by the power of your name—the name you gave me—so that they may be one as we are one" (John 17:11, NIV).

One? The longer I stayed in Taiwan, the more I realized that we had a serious problem with oneness. Missionaries had attacked each other with machetes. Some hardly spoke to one another. I attended one Sabbath school where a minor question—was the war in heaven mental or physical?—seemed to bring a few missionaries to the verge of spontaneous combustion.

When I was young, I would wonder how, with all those missionaries and all those mission dollars, we still hadn't managed to baptize all the world. Now, actually looking at our missions, I wondered how we managed to baptize *anyone*. *Truly,* I thought when I saw new converts, *God's spirit is working on these people, because their conversion certainly isn't our doing.*

Yet I knew that God's presence did not excuse our lack of unity. After a month in my own mission, I discovered that living with two guys and one Chinese lady gets lonely. I discovered that Aaron could make some terribly unkind comments without thinking. I discovered that Derek didn't know some Bible stories that I had known since infancy. I'm sure I seemed to them a finicky recluse, requiring far too much time alone (aren't all missionaries supposed to thrive on human presence 24 hours a day, seven days a week?) and spending an absurd amount of time answering e-mail.

Jody, our registrar, was as faithful and kind a human being as I have ever met. However, I learned, unhappily, that she could not fill the place that my girlfriends had filled at home. We were too different.

One? How could we possibly be one?

I remember one day being furious with Aaron for making a joke about Jody that I considered cruel. I sat in my room and fumed. Then suddenly it hit me: *Satan is laughing right now. Our little school will never function to save souls if we despise each other. I can sit here and be angry, or I can go to Aaron and try to fix it.*

I didn't want to go. Confrontation was never my strong point. But I prayed, and I went.

After a few hours' talking I discovered that my fellow missionary was not only capable of graciously accepting criticism, but was genuinely concerned that he might have hurt someone. We got along better after that. He tried not to joke so thoughtlessly, and I tried not to assume the worst.

And Derek? Derek had a capacity for tolerating human company that astounded me. Long after I had retreated to my room in exhaustion, he was still talking to students, trying to speak Chinese (and eventually succeeding), playing Ping-Pong, and letting them come into every crevice of his living space. As he began to give Bible studies, he had questions, and the answers (as I pointed out) were in books. By the time we left, he was reading quite a lot, and I was tolerating masses of people far better than ever before.

What happened? What changed after the first shaky month? We were male and female, Chinese and American, from eastern and western parts of the country, of different ages, with different careers in front of us. Yet within a short time we were one of the few schools that seemed to have no interpersonal problems at all. Where one of us was weak, another was strong. Where one of us lacked proportion, another provided balance.

Our unity certainly didn't come from outward similarity. Was it merely superhuman effort and altruism that made our school function?

I don't think so. The Bible says that the Spirit of God is the source of unity in the body of Christ. "The body is a unit, though it is made up of many parts; and though all its parts are many, they form one body. So it is with Christ. For we were all baptized by one Spirit into one body—whether Jews or Greeks, slave or free—and we were all given the one Spirit to drink" (1 Corinthians 12:12, 13, NIV). Like organs in a human body, God used the missionaries in my school to fill different roles—not to contradict, but to complement and improve.

As far as I know, there had been no baptisms in our town before we came. However, four of the people with whom we worked were baptized soon after I left. Praise God! His Spirit, not ours, made this possible. Unity in the body of Christ is a result of unity of faith and purpose, not of outward similarity.

But this leaves one nagging issue. I encountered it soon after my arrival in Taiwan while I was talking to a pastor of another denomination, who had attended one of our church functions.

His appearance at such events was not uncommon. As far as I know, there are only three major Christian denominations in Taiwan. The country is vastly pagan, with Christians composing only

10 percent of the population. Idol worship, supernatural manifestation by demons, paralyzing superstition, the worship of ghosts and spirits—these things are rampant. My tiny town had a temple on almost every street.

Standing beside these ancient religions, all denominations of Christianity seem very similar. I remember trying to explain to a confused student that not all Christians are alike. I tried to explain denominational differences and felt a wave of embarrassment, realizing that to him the differences sounded tremendously petty.

And yet what this pastor said disturbed me. He said: "We're all on the same side here, all Christians alike!"

No! I wanted to say to him. *No, we're not! We Adventists have the third angel's message, we have the Sabbath, we have the dead in the right place, we have . . . unity? In the body of Christ?*

But what is the body of Christ? Just Adventists?

It's a hard question, because when the New Testament was written, there was only one official Christian denomination. I recalled to myself the incident when the disciples wanted to silence a man who was not of their number and yet was healing in the name of Jesus. Christ told them to let him alone, "for whoever is not against us is for us" (Mark 9:40, NIV).

Although there were no separately organized Christian denominations in John's day, the churches of Ephesus, Smyrna, Pergamum, Thyatira, Sardis, Philadelphia, and Laodicea were so different that he wrote completely different advice to them. Paul and Peter clashed so fiercely over some of their theology that they couldn't be around one another. Yet they all considered themselves (and each other) part of the body of Christ. After Jesus had finished praying for the twelve, He went on to say, "My prayer is not for them alone. I pray also for those who will believe in me through their message, that all of them may be one, Father, just as you are in me and I am in you" (John 17:20, 21, NIV).

Looking at that pastor, I squirmed at admitting unity with him, yet I could not reasonably convince myself that God would not bless his efforts.

Thankfully I do not have to judge whose work to bless and whose to leave in the outer darkness. That is God's job. In the meantime I can work for unity in my own mission, at home or abroad.

No matter what part we play in the body of Christ, I think we can all agree with David when he said: "How good and pleasant it is when brothers live together in unity!" (Ps. 133:1, NIV).

1. Have you ever had difficulty with unity in your own church? If so, how was the problem resolved?
2. Do you think that the question of unity is as important as other fundamental Adventist beliefs? Why or why not?
3. The splintered face of Christianity is discouraging to nonbelievers. They see this as evidence that there is nothing special about our religion. What would you say to a pagan friend (a civilized, modern person) who has doubts about Christianity based on its lack of unity?
4. Define "body of Christ." Could "body" be a different category from "denomination" or "church"? Why or why not?
5. Do you believe that God blesses missionaries from churches besides your own?
6. Recall a time you managed to achieve unity with someone with whom you did not at first get along. How was this accomplished?
7. Is there any danger in the idea of unity? Can it be carried to an extreme?
8. How can we keep a balanced perspective on unity in the body of Christ?

Abbie Hilton, 23, is a senior preveterinary student at Southern Adventist University. Her home is in Avon Park, Florida, with her parents, little brother, two dogs, and three cats (one of which is a rescued Taiwanese street cat). Abbie enjoys reading, writing, scuba diving, racquetball, and taxidermy.

14

BAPTISM

Shasta Burr

Why Should I Care?
Baptism is the sign of a believer's new life in Christ.

How Can I Know?

Mark 16:16

John 3:5

Ephesians 4:5

Matthew 3:13-17

Mark 1:9, 10

Colossians 2:12

Romans 6:3-6

Acts 2:38

I Corinthians 12:13

Acts 22:16

With her beautiful black hair all twisted up high, her big red hoop earrings hanging from her ears, and the slight smell of cigarette smoke lingering on her clothes, I sensed this was her first time in a church for a while. She tentatively slid past me and sat on the pew smiling sweetly and warmly at those around her, yet her eyes told of unknown emptiness. It was an emptiness that revealed to me a hunger for the things that I knew only God could fill, and I silently prayed that she might realize that too. Taking a deep breath, I moved to introduce myself and hand her the materials for that evening's meetings. That night something stirred in me: I wanted more than anything for God to fill this young woman in a powerful way.

She listened intensely that evening, sitting forward in her seat as though the words were being said directly to her. She came back night after night. A few evenings later she asked us for a ride home, as she and her children had apparently walked the distance that evening and it was very late and dark outside. As my husband entertained her children and brought laughter to their eyes, the young woman began to flood me with the questions of her heart.

I can't even describe the fear that clutched my own heart as we talked. *Do I know the answers to these questions? What if I say the wrong thing? What if I turn her away?* Silently I begged God to give me the right words to say. But today I can't even recall that conversation . . . somehow God told her whatever she needed to hear. She seemed so ready to give her life to God.

Or so I thought. After our conversation she missed an entire week of the meetings, so I found myself at her run-down house seven days later, knocking on the beaten door. I didn't know what had caused her to miss all the meetings, but when she tentatively opened her door to invite us in, her lips shared her story.

Regret filled the words she spoke to us, revealing the pain that people encounter only when they are addicted to cocaine. "For five years I've tried to quit," she told us brokenly. "But it's been impossible." We learned that she had relapsed this weekend. It had been an ugly time, filled with tears, bruises, and hate-filled words. She wanted so badly to live a life in Jesus, but it seemed far outside of her reach. And I hated to admit it, but she was right. For her, Christianity did seem impossible. We needed a miracle.

My husband and I knelt in that home with her and her two children, and together we all prayed for a miracle. We all knew that she could try desperately to be a better person, but it would never be enough. As we prayed, God gave us the miracle we asked for. It was as if He said to us: "You're right; I am outside of your reach, all of you. But the miracle is that I have reached down as far as it takes to touch you. All you have to do is choose to take My hand."

She decided that she wanted to experience baptism and work toward building her relationship with Jesus regardless of her sin. Her sins were covered by the blood of Jesus—no matter what they were.

In fact, we studied Romans 7 and 8 and discovered that baptism is a miracle itself, since the same power that fills one with the Spirit at baptism also raised Jesus from the dead.

Her eyes filled with an understanding of God's character and grace that came not from knowledge, but from experience. Before me sat a woman who lived God's grace, experienced His love, and requested His power. He entered her life right then and there. We had received our miracle.

The next night she returned to the meetings. Her life was changed, and she was committed to living a life that glorified God. Her understanding expanded, and her habits changed when she felt convicted by God to change them. Her children learned to pray, and she made a fresh resolution to be clean from drugs—with the help of her rehabilitation program and her relationship with Christ. She was the same woman, yet she was different.

Her name is Netta. Actually it is Angelnetta, but everyone calls her Netta. I will never forget her. In just six weeks she had become a completely different person. She walked into that baptismal tank with a confidence that few possess as they step into cool water. Her chin was straight with pride, and her eyes stared ahead as she followed through on the biggest decision of her life. Her children, ages 6 and 8, stood beside me, smiling at the woman their mom had become. It was the most beautiful of all moments.

There is power in baptism, in surrendering one's life to God. Notwithstanding all of our sins and bad habits, God says, "You are still mine, and I will wash you as white as snow as soon as you want it." We accept that gift of purity in a public way when we are baptized as Christians.

My own baptism was powerful and meaningful, but there is *nothing* that has touched me in my Christian journey like being involved in bringing someone God loves back to Him. Watching a person symbolically die to self as they are completely immersed into water and be raised back to life by His power can take your breath away. Baptism is a miracle available to anyone who wants it.

Netta made this miracle real to me. I witnessed a true-life story of how God transforms people. Before, the doctrine of baptism was merely that—a doctrine. Now I see the doctrine as the words that attempt to describe a power, a gift, a miracle that God gives to us, His children.

But just like me, you will never understand this doctrine by studying it—it's truly by experiencing it in your own life and witnessing it in others that you can thank God for such a beautiful, life-changing biblical truth.

Praise God for answering our prayer for a miracle . . . 2,000 years before we ever knelt to ask for it.

1. What motivates people to make major changes in their lives?

2. What do you think are some of the major misconceptions about baptism that the devil has allowed to permeate our society? What does the true biblical baptism reveal about Christ's character?

3. Read about Jesus' baptism in Matthew 3:13-17 and answer the following questions:

Why was Jesus baptized? Was it to cleanse Him from sin?

What do we tell the world by being baptized?

If God spoke in audible voice about you today, as He did about Jesus, what might He say?

4. Read Romans 7:7-25, which highlights our battle with sin, and answer the following questions:

How have you experienced a struggle with sin similar to what Paul describes?

What hope do we have of deliverance from sin here on earth?

How can knowing that God has achieved the ultimate victory over sin affect your prayers, thoughts, and attitudes?

5. Now read Romans 6:1-14, which illustrates to us the power of Christ's victory and gift of baptism, and answer the following questions:

What does baptism symbolize about our relationship with Christ?

How will uniting with Christ in His death change the future of our lives?

How do you think God helps a person discard old and ugly habits and tendencies?

What kind of changes does God want to make in our lives when we become Christians?

How can you actively resist the tendency to sin in your everyday life with whatever temptation you are currently fighting?

Shasta Burr, 23, was baptized when she was 13 years old. She and her husband, Jerry, live in downtown Seattle, Washington, where she is an associate pastor for a church plant that hopes to baptize and give new meaning to life for those who live in the city.

15

THE LORD'S SUPPER
James A. Dittes

Why Should I Care?

As He served His disciples and ate with them, Christ founded a tradition that His followers could not help imitating—and appreciating.

How Can I Know?

Deuteronomy 26:11

Exodus 24:8

Psalm 116:13,17

Psalm 40:6-8

Exodus 16

Matthew 26:28, 29

Mark 14:12-28,
    see also Matthew 26:17-31

Luke 22:24-30

John 13:1-17

John 6:32-40

Acts 2:42

Acts 20:7

Acts 2:46, 47

1 Corinthians 10:14-17

1 Corinthians 11:23-26

1 Corinthians 11:26

During the NATO-Yugoslav war in 1999 I served with ADRA (Adventist Development and Relief Agency) in Albania, distributing food to Kosovar refugees living in camps scattered throughout the country's southwest. With their homeland in ruins and ravaged by years of war, the refugees moved into shelters hastily arranged by the Albanian government. The lucky ones lived with local host families; the rest settled in makeshift warehouses, school dormitories, and abandoned hotels.

One of those so-called camps was in Divjakë (div-YAH-kuh), a seaside village on the Adriatic Sea, where a state-run Hotel Tourizm had been converted to house more than 900 refugees. The six-story main building dominated the camp and housed about 400 of the refugees in its 24 rooms (about 18 residents per room—a common ratio throughout the crisis). The remaining refugees lived in a line of one-room beach shacks, separated from the sea by a 100-yard beach.

While most people wouldn't mind a summer at the beach, the mood of the Kosovars I visited there was always dour. Although we distributed tons of food and fresh vegetables every week, there were always complaints: babies needed milk, some men wanted cigarettes, no one had enough meat. This converted resort must have been strange indeed to these mountain people, who had probably never before seen the sea.

One day I arranged to meet the delivery truck at Divjakë following a meeting in the nearby town of Lushnje (Lushnia). The meeting got out late, and I hurried along in my 4x4 to meet the truck, only to find upon my arrival that the delivery was even later than I was. As I waited I spoke with some of the refugees I had met on an earlier visit. We spoke of the war, of our homelands, and when they learned that my workers were late, they invited me to their room.

From the beginning of my sojourn in Albania I had been overwhelmed by the Albanians' refined sense of hospitality. It was not uncommon for an Albanian family, subsisting on an income of $40 a month, to host a Kosovar family of six to 11 members. Plus, every celebration, business decision, or discussion there took place around a meal. "I need to talk with you about something" was invariably followed with the words, "Let's find a place to eat."

As I followed my Kosovar friends to their room, this customary hospitality came to mind. *I won't accept any food,* I thought to myself. *After all, who is feeding whom here?* Yet from the moment that I stepped through the door, I was served. There was nothing I could do about it.

Within moments someone offered me a bottle of water, and I sat down with the Kosovars to learn about their hometown of Gjakova and share details of my home in Arizona. A few minutes later the mother of the house appeared with a plate of rice garnished with cucumbers. Atop the steaming rice was a cooked chicken leg.

I was humbled, for I knew how difficult it was for these poor, homeless people to acquire meat. I knew how priceless this delicacy would seem to the dozens of Kosovars around me. *I can't,* I thought. *It costs too much.*

I accepted the meal, though. It may have been difficult for a Kosovar to get chicken, but it was infinitely more difficult to reject such a gift. Squatting there on donated woolen blankets in a building that was little more than a hovel, I ate in the presence of my friends, and relished the most luxurious meal of my life.

It was a meal I hadn't expected and didn't deserve—the only meal I would ever eat with those friends, who returned to Kosovo just three weeks later. I remain, even now, in debt for their hospitality. With little hope of repaying them, I am left to simply emulate: to give of my home, my rice, my priceless chicken leg.

Forgiveness, like the Kosovar's hospitality, is another such priceless gift that simply cannot be given back. Adventists and all other Christian denominations regularly celebrate the night that forgiveness became ours through the ceremony of the Lord's Supper.

At the Last Supper Christ, in His final night of life on earth, chose a simple meal to leave the most profound lessons with His friends. They were much like me that special evening in Divjakë: self-righteous do-gooders, just waiting for their big reward. James and John imagined themselves coprefects in Christ's soon-to-come earthly kingdom. No doubt others had already chosen provinces they would rule or armies they would lead against the Romans.

Christ had no sword with which to grant knighthood to His disciples. Instead He took a towel and washed their feet. His sole mark of power was a washbasin. Just days earlier, in fact, this very role had featured a former prostitute!

Then Christ did something He had done from the beginning of His ministry. He broke bread. He drank wine. Only this time He said, "Remember Me." For those in the upper room that night, no loaf of bread—leavened or unleavened—would be broken again without the thought of their Friend who awaited them in heaven. For those disciples, and we who follow in their steps, wine would be a bitter drink until Christ passed the cup to each of His friends in His Father's kingdom.

There were no waiters at the Last Supper, no attendants, probably no dishwashers either. Christ took care of everything that night, and He offers to serve us likewise today. All we have to do is wash ourselves, eat, and drink—and in doing these ordinary things, remember Him.

The sacrifice of Christ's life was a gift that I couldn't have expected and certainly don't deserve. I accept it anyway. I learned from the Kosovars the luxury and comfort—not to mention the friendship—that comes from such a gift.

1. What was the "new covenant" established between Christ and His followers at the Last Supper (Luke 22:20)? How did it relate to the covenants God established with Abraham (Genesis 15:18) and Moses (Exodus 24:8)?

2. Is the foot-washing ceremony really a necessary prelude to Communion? After all, most Christian churches do not follow this procedure. Does it expand our understanding of the service as a whole?

3. When we eat the bread and drink the wine, we are sharing in Christ's sacrifice of His own life. Is there any further sacrifice expected of us?

4. What would you have said if Christ offered to wash your feet? Would you have drunk wine that He said represented His blood?

5. The disciples mistakenly expected Christ to set up an earthly kingdom the night of Passover. Is there a place for Christians among the earthly kingdoms of today? Based on Christ's example, what are we empowered to do?

6. Is there a way the Communion service could be made more meaningful? What are some songs, locations, prayers that would amplify the meaning of this sacred ceremony?

7. With the Lord's Supper as a starting point, examine the Crucifixion and the Resurrection. What was the mood Christ was trying to evoke among His disciples as He ate with them? Cautious? Optimistic? Bittersweet? (Hint: each Gospel brings out a different side of Christ's purpose.)

James A. Dittes, 29, lives in Westmoreland, Tennessee, with his wife, Jenny. He is a full-time father to Ellie, 3, and newborn son, Owen. His writing has been published in Adventist Review, Primary Treasure, *and* Collegiate Quarterly.

16

SPIRITUAL GIFTS AND MINISTRIES

Stephanie Swilley

Why Should I care?
God gives everyone talents and abilities that make us special and provide a way for us to support His ministry and support one another.

How Can I Know?

Romans 12:4-8

1 Corinthians 12:9-11, 27, 28

Ephesians 4:8, 11-16

Acts 6:1-7

1 Timothy 3:1-13

1 Peter 4:10, 11

Galatians 5:22-26

1 Corinthians 14:1, 37

Romans 1:11, 12

Hebrews 2:1-4

Ephesians 1:3-6

2 Corinthians 8:7

Galatians 3:1-5

Colossians 1:15-18, 24

1 Corinthians 6:19, 20

2 Corinthians 5:17-20

Ephesians 2:10

Philippians 2:1-4

James 3:15, 16

N ear the end of my junior year of college I decided on a whim that, yeah, OK, being editor of the school newspaper would be a great experience.

I gave it serious thought, which meant calling my mom and sister, hoping they would tell me what to do. They were no help, giving me only more questions, such as "Well, what do *you* want to do?" and "What would make you happy?" In the end my inability to say no forced me to take the job.

Immediately I wondered what in the world I was thinking.

Sure, I'd love to crank out a 12-page paper full of campus news each week. Sure, I'd love to spend every waking moment thinking about copy and layout. Sure, I'd love to beg people week in and week out to *please* write for me. How hard could that be?

The semester ended, and summer rolled around. I put the paper out of my mind and went on to my summer job. But little fears kept creeping up from the back of my mind.

What if I can't put together a staff? What if the students hate my paper? What if it's obvious I don't know what I'm doing?

The what ifs were killing me, and I did my best to put them out of my mind and have fun. But eventually it was time to head back to good ol' Southern Adventist University and get ready for my last year as a college student.

Since I had no delusions of grandeur, I was fully aware that I really didn't know anything about putting a newspaper out each week. So my first priority was to get a great staff. I shamelessly bribed the people I wanted, using all the tactics that had worked on me. *Think of the experience! You'll meet so many new people! It really won't take much time out of your week!*

I gave out pizza, great titles, and access to our homey office, which had a TV. With cable. I laid guilt trips on anyone I even remotely knew and promised they would get paid. Inevitably, these irritatingly curious journalists wanted to know how much. After I whispered the pitifully low sum, they laughed, and I was back to begging and laying guilt trips.

Surprisingly, lots of people signed up to help. Feeling much more optimistic, I faced our first production night with great cheer and enthusiasm. We were doing only eight pages. The night was young. I wondered, *How hard could this be?*

Much of that night has been reduced to a blur in my memory, but I do recall calling a friend around 1:00 a.m., crying and wondering if we would ever finish. Only one page was put together, and who knew how long the rest would take? Apparently, I called the wrong friend, because with little sympathy he ordered me back to work, saying, "You're the one who wanted to do this, remember?" At least my anger helped wake me up. I downed a Dr. Pepper, got a hold on my waning patience, and returned to my small army of helpers.

By some great miracle we did finish the pages and headed back to our rooms around 7:00 a.m. Just in time to get ready for 8:00 a.m. class.

This was not to be the last all-nighter trying to get the *Southern Accent* out. Every Tuesday night a little band of five could be found slaving over photos, stories, and layouts. And every week I was shocked and amazed that these students, who surely had other, better things to do, gave so much time and energy to our cause.

Each staff member brought special talents to our newspaper. I looked to Hans for all things computer-related. To his credit, he did try to teach me some stuff, but I mostly just smiled and nodded my head, hoping he would handle it all. Kelly was the photo queen and had the amazing ability to round up a photo of anything just as I was starting to panic. Kerensa had more design talent in one fingertip than I had in my whole body. When something looked awful, she could turn it into a work of art in under five minutes. And keeping us all sane was cool, calm Robin. Nothing rattled her, and boy, was that nice as tempers started to flare around 3:00 a.m.

And then there were the regular guests who, for some inexplicable reason, actually *enjoyed* staying up all night with us. Whatever their reasons, we looked forward to their arrival. They kept us laughing, brought food, and made the whole night much more fun.

A job that was a greater endeavor than I had ever imagined was made bearable, and even occasionally enjoyable, by my talented staff. I came to realize that each of these people had necessary skills that I lacked, and I needed all of them in order to get the job done.

Romans 12 says, "In Christ we who are many form one body, and each member belongs to all the others" (verse 5, NIV). Each member has a different function, but we are all to work together.

If you're like me, you're forever wondering, "What is my spiritual gift?" When I think of gifts, I move into Christmas list mode, mentally preparing my wish list. But God doesn't give me a new skirt or the latest CD—He gives gifts of far more value. He bestows talents and abilities that make me unique. From my stint as editor, I realized that I'm a good organizer. I'm obsessive enough to remember all the little details. And I really like being in charge.

I'd rather have a tooth pulled than give a sermon or go door to door selling anything, but I applaud those who have those talents. Fortunately, God doesn't make us all do the same thing. "There are different kinds of service, but the same Lord" (1 Corinthians 12:5, NIV). God makes room for every type of skill, whether it's in computers, music, or public speaking.

When you find what floats your boat, look for a way to serve God with it. Remember that song lyric—"Hide it under a bushel? No!"? There's no reason to hide your light. Use it to build up your church, friends, or anyone else looking to find their light.

Fear not. God has given *you* unique talents. Nurture them, develop them, and by all means, use them.

1. What do you think are your spiritual talents?
2. How can you *know* what they are?
3. How can you use them to help God and others?
4. Why do you think God gave you these abilities?
5. Does He give talents to everyone? Even non-Christians?
6. What happens to talents if you don't use them?
7. Do you think some people have more talents than others?
8. Healing, prophesying, and speaking in tongues are listed as spiritual gifts (see 1 Corinthians 12:8-11; 14). Do people still have them today?
9. Are some talents more important than others?

Stephanie Swilley, 22, recently graduated from Southern Adventist University in Collegedale, Tennessee, with a degree in public relations. She now lives in Nashville, Tennessee, and in addition to her other talents, she excels at procrastination, worrying, and spending way too much money on clothes.

17

THE GIFT OF PROPHECY

Julie Hill Alvarez

Why Should I Care?

Understanding God's gift of prophecy helps me to appreciate His use of modern-day prophets.

How Can I Know?

Numbers 12:6

2 Chronicles 20:20

Joel 2:28, 29

Amos 3:7

Matthew 24:24

Acts 2:14-21

Romans 12:6

1 Thessalonians 5:19-22

Revelation 12:17

Revelation 19:10

California will disappear into the Pacific Ocean in 1995 . . . The battle of Armageddon is now taking place in Jordan . . . New messiah to be born in Rio de Janeiro . . . Ronald Wilson Reagan has the mark of the beast because there are six letters in each of his names . . . Elvis will be seen again at Graceland after all his memorabilia has been returned . . .

When most people hear the word *prophecy,* the first things they think of are the predictions screaming from grocery store tabloids. A prophet is perceived as a crazy con artist whose title should be spelled with an *f* instead of a *ph*. However, this twisted view of prophets and prophecy does not change God's genuine, precious gift of prophecy. God's intention is that prophets speak for Him. He chooses individuals to convey the infinities of His love in human terms because we are His tenderly molded creations, and His heart longs for a relationship with us.

The position of prophet is not a vocation based on heredity, education, or popular election. God has always called His own prophets. A prophet can be from any country, culture, or economic background. Physical characteristics and gender are unimportant. A prophet's principle work is to communicate God's message to His people.

Throughout the centuries God has set apart men and women to be His prophets. The Bible shares the lives of more than 275 of them. Wealthy Abraham and his prosperous family became wanderers in a foreign land before becoming the race through whom God planned to reveal Himself to the world (see Genesis 12). God gave the Ten Commandments to Egyptian prince Moses as he led the children of Israel (see Exodus 20). Judge Deborah not only ruled and gave religious instruction from God; she also led the Israelites to a great victory over their enemies (see Judges 4; 5). Samuel was only a young boy when God gave him a message for Eli the priest (see 1 Samuel 3). Brave Nathan showed King David his great sin of killing Uriah, the husband of Bathsheba (see 2 Samuel 12). Ehud, the left-handed prophet, stuck his sword into the belly of the idolater, King Eglon (see Judges 3). Isaiah spent 60 years calling for a prosperous people to realize their need of God (see Isaiah). Builder Ezra led the Israelites in restoring the temple in Jerusalem (see Ezra 3). Ordained by God before his birth, John the Baptist prepared people for the earthly ministry of Jesus (see Luke 1:57-80). Widow Anna recognized Baby Jesus in the Temple and announced the Child as the Messiah (see Luke 2:36). Fisherman Peter and tentmaker Paul continue to lead and guide the Christian church today through their writings.

I believe that God continues to call prophets to instruct, rebuke, and reveal through the centuries. One of these modern-day prophets became real to me in college.

It was a Saturday, and I was eating lunch with friends in the college cafeteria and discussing our afternoon plans. Some were headed to relax at the beach, others to hike around a lake, and some to take a much-needed nap. Gina said that she was going to be a tour guide at the national historic house of Elmshaven. My curiosity was piqued: Why would a 19-year-old volunteer her free afternoon to guide hordes of people through a creaky old house? I asked her, and she invited me to come and take the tour for myself.

After lunch and a change of clothes several friends and I squeezed into my white Honda and headed five miles down a winding, tree-lined road. My first view of Elmshaven was of a large two-story white clapboard house with many tall windows and a well-tended yard. Along the path to the front door were fragrant roses, forget-me-nots, and a welcome drinking fountain.

We walked onto the front porch and rang the doorbell. Next to the door was a plaque that read: "Elmshaven, home of author Ellen G. White, has been designated a national landmark. This site possesses national significance in commemorating the history of the United States of America."

My friend Gina greeted us at the door. Immediately inside to my left I could see a beautiful wooden staircase. A doorway to my right led to a parlor, and a room straight ahead was lined with glass display cases full of memorabilia. Gina started our tour among the memorabilia by telling us that she herself is the great-great-great granddaughter of Ellen White, who handwrote more than 100,000 pages on a variety of topics and is considered by some people to be a modern-day prophet. She then showed us Ellen White's Seventh-day Adventist ministerial license, typewritten manuscript pages edited in her own hand, and copies of the more than 26 books she wrote in more than 70 years of ministry. On the walls were photographs of such institutions as Loma Linda University (a medical school in southern California), Paradise Valley Hospital (a private hospital in Escondido, California), Avondale College (a Christian college in Australia), and Pacific Union College (a Christian college in the Napa Valley), that she helped to found.

In the parlor we saw the original furniture where the family gathered morning and evening for worship. Even the pump organ that was played to accompany their hymn singing was still there. Blue and white tiles around the fireplace depicted scenes from King

Arthur's court. Gina told us that Ellen White created stories about these tiles to entertain her visiting grandchildren.

Food was an integral part of the White household. The dining room was connected to the parlor and had a huge table in it. Apparently Ellen White invited anyone who was in the house to stay for dinner. Her cook never knew how much food to prepare and always set all 10 places at the table. Ellen's family joked that her house was a free hotel. I learned that she ate a healthful vegetarian diet that included a wide range of fruits and vegetables, fresh milk and eggs, and even some cake now and again. While she herself felt best eating two meals a day, she did not impose this restriction on her household, and there was always food on the big table for those who needed it.

Next to the dining room were the kitchen and pantry. The kitchen had a wood-burning cookstove, a table, an ironing board, and a birdcage in the corner. Gina said that Ellen White enjoyed the cheerful sounds of the birds singing. By looking at the kitchen, I could tell why Ellen White needed a cook. There was no microwave, refrigerator, or gas oven. If she had cooked for her family, she wouldn't have had time to write or do other forms of ministry. The kitchen had many doors. I found most interesting the one that led up the back way to her writing room.

The narrow, steep staircase was a favorite way for Ellen White's grandchildren to sneak up and visit her while she was working. They loved to come and tell her stories about their explorations in the barnyard and orchards. She often had an apple or special treat for them.

Ellen White's writing room was an awe-inspiring place. I stood there and looked around this space where God's messenger (she preferred this title over "prophet") had handwritten pages of counsel, admonition, guidance, and descriptions of the battle between good and evil—Christ and Satan. Lots of windows allowed light for writing during the day, and a fireplace and oil lamps for writing during the night. One of the two comfortable-looking chairs in the room had a foldable writing desk and a footrest attached. I could almost picture Ellen White sitting there writing with her quill pen.

Just outside the writing room was the hallway that led to her bedroom. It was in this hallway that Ellen White tripped and fell, breaking her hip. This fall eventually led to her death in July 1915 at age 87.

Gina said that Ellen White received most of her messages from God in her bedroom. I stood in the room, looking at the high wooden bed and the beautiful butterfly picture on the wall (given to her by the Australian people when she left Australia), and thought about what an interesting person this woman was.

Ellen Gould Harmon was given her first message from God in December 1844 at age 17. In this vision she saw the people of God walking up a narrow path to heaven with their eyes fixed on Jesus. With this message she encouraged a handful of eager Bible seekers (who later became the Seventh-day Adventist Church) that they were on the right path. She married her good friend James White in 1846. In 1851 her first book, *A Sketch of the Christian Experience and Views of Ellen G. White,* was published. Over her 70-year ministry she had more than 2,000 visions and wrote 26 books, 5,000 articles, 200 tracts and pamphlets, and 6,000 typewritten documents consisting of letters and general manuscripts.

Anyone who personally reads her writings in context sees that her primary focus was pointing people to Jesus. She passionately longed for every person to have a continually deepening relationship with Jesus. She was not afraid to point out things that hold people back from this intimate friendship. Her book *Steps to Christ,* which describes how to walk with Jesus, has been translated into more than 100 languages and is the most widely read devotional book in history.

"By their fruit you will recognize them" (Matthew 7:20, NIV). When the life of Ellen White is examined, she fulfills every Biblical qualification of a prophet (see footnote). She compared her writings and the Bible to the relationship between the moon and the sun. As the "lesser light," her writings have nothing in them that is not a reflection of the Bible. However, she realized that some people were skeptical of her as a prophet. She said that a belief in her as a divinely inspired messenger of God was not to be a test of fellowship for joining the Seventh-day Adventist Church.

That day at Elmshaven I came to see Ellen White as a real, caring person with a sense of humor who was well liked by the people around her. When I returned to my college dorm room, I decided to read something that she wrote. I went to a bookstore and bought her book *The Desire of Ages,* about the life of Jesus Christ. I read it in conjunction with a study of the Gospel of Matthew. My understanding of the life of Christ increased and my devotional time became more meaningful as I saw Christ's ministry from a fresh perspective. Since then I have read many more of her books and found that each of them has helped my relationship with Christ to grow.

God does not want to remain a mystery to humankind. By using prophets throughout history, He has presented a clearer picture of Himself. He is a loving God who wants to be in a personal relationship with each one. His prophets through the ages have guided individuals to Him—and continue to do so today.

1. How do you feel about the gift of prophecy?
2. Do you believe that there could be prophets of God now?
3. Why do you think Jesus speaks through prophets?
4. How would you feel if someone told you that he or she was a prophet?
5. How can you tell if someone is a true prophet?
6. In what ways can you use the writings of Ellen White to gain a greater understanding of the Bible?
7. What specific effort do you think Jesus wants you to make in order to grow in a relationship with Him?

Biblical tests of prophets

1. Deuteronomy 18:9-14—will have nothing to do with the occult
2. Isaiah 8:20—will agree with the Bible
3. 1 John 4:2, 3—will teach the divinity and humanity of Christ
4. Matthew 7:15-23—will bear positive fruit
5. Deuteronomy 18:22; Jeremiah 28:9—predictive prophecies will be accurately fulfilled
6. Jeremiah 18:7-10—conditional element of predictive prophecies.

Julie Hill Alvarez, 23, is moving to Orlando, Florida (the land of sun), from Auburn, Washington (the land of rain), where she has been the youth pastor at Auburn Adventist Academy. She enjoys developing the talents of youth for leadership in their church. Cooking, traveling, mission trips, reading, and e-mailing are among her hobbies. She lives with her fabulous husband, Hector, and their two Garfield cats (Scratch and Sniff). She has her nursing degree from Pacific Union College (where her little brother Tim is now going to college).

18

THE LAW OF GOD
Kellie Van Eyk

Why Should I Care?
Believing and living the law of God gives me true freedom.

How Can I Know?

Exodus 20:1-17	John 15:7-10
Psalm 40:7	Ephesians 2:8-10
Matthew 22:36-40	1 John 5:3
Deuteronomy 28:1-14	Romans 9:31-33
Matthew 5:17-20	Psalm 19:7-14
Hebrews 8:8-10	Psalm 119:47

It was a gang initiation. He had to do this to prove he was a man. Shots were fired and the elderly woman dropped to the ground. *She was old. Who cares?* he thought. "THOU SHALT NOT KILL."

She wouldn't let him hurt them again. This time he had come home drunk and attempted to slap their infant son. With shaking hands she pointed the gun at him. "This is the last time you'll hurt us," she said, pulling the trigger. "THOU SHALT NOT KILL."

She had a loving husband and two beautiful children. For some reason, though, she missed the thrill of late-night parties and wild dating. One night she went out on the town with the girls. She ended up meeting a young man and sleeping with him. She knew it was wrong, but it sure was fun. "THOU SHALT NOT COMMIT ADULTERY."

It had been so long since her husband told her he loved her. She begged him to take some time off work to spend with her. He refused every time, making excuses to stay at work longer each night. Why didn't he love her anymore? Did he no longer find her attractive? Then she met a man at the gym. This man told her everything she longed to hear. An affair followed. "THOU SHALT NOT COMMIT ADULTERY."

He didn't care anymore. He desperately needed the money for drugs. The purse was lying there, unattended. He took it. "THOU SHALT NOT STEAL."

At age 12 he was now head of the household. Dad died two years ago. Mom tried to work when she could, but there were two other children to look after. His family was so hungry. Then he saw the wallet, left on a park bench. He took it. "THOU SHALT NOT STEAL."

Do you feel the same dilemma I do about the above situations? Are all the people in the above stories equally guilty of breaking the corresponding commandment? Is God's law set in stone, or does it vary by circumstance and situation? Did Adam and Eve deserve to be cast out of a beautiful garden paradise for breaking only one command of God? What exactly is the purpose of the law of God? Is it merely to condemn those who have done wrong and set them straight? How is the law related to grace—or is it? Are there really "gray" areas in life, or is everything black and white to God?

My 21-year-old cousin, Christopher, hated to be late to work. But one morning last year he got to the railroad tracks just as the crossing guards went down. He maneuvered his Lincoln Continental between the gates as he had many times before . . . only this time he didn't make it. There was nothing the train engineer could do. Even though Christopher had good intentions, he suffered the same consequences that anyone trying to beat a train could face.

I have had this same experience with sin. For about a year I struggled with a personal sin that I cherished. I knew it was wrong, but had no intention of giving it up, because I loved it too much. Unfortunately, the longer I continued in this sin, the more I lost the ability to detect that it was actually sin. Eventually my actions actually started to seem not so bad to me. I became just as comfortable with this sin as Chris was with beating oncoming trains. In his book *The Life You've Always Wanted* John Ortberg says, "Sin carries with it a certain moral myopia. . . . It distorts our ability to detect its presence." That is exactly what happened to me.

But it couldn't go on forever. Even though I had broken God's law hundreds of times without results, the consequences of my sin eventually caught up with me. My family, my friends, and I were hurt by my choices. Since that experience I have come to believe that God's law is actually very kind. The heartache I have endured could have been avoided. God *wanted* me to avoid it. I, however, ignored the people who tried to warn me. I even went as far as calling them "self-righteous" for pointing out my sin. But God wants me (and all humanity) to be truly free from the consequences of sin.

God's law is often a dilemma to us because sin is so much fun! Can't God simply change the terrible consequences of sin so we can have more fun? Such is the great controversy between God and Satan. Satan had freedom of choice, and he used it to attack the fairness of God's law. Now he is suffering the consequences of his sin. God has given each of us that same freedom of choice. But that won't keep Him from reaching out to us to try to save us from ourselves.

When I was 9 my parents divorced; a couple years later my mom remarried. After studying, my mom and stepdad became Seventh-day Adventists. I was sent to an Adventist church school, academy, and then college. In the Adventist Church I learned a lot about the law of God. I memorized it, recited it, tried to live it, and got frustrated with it. During those years there was a controversy in the church over the relationship of grace to the law. It appeared to me that there were two camps of people. One group believed you kept the law on your own strength and willpower, based on your knowledge of the law. The other group seemed to believe that all you had to do was love God, and His grace would make it easy to keep the law. I was young, and I remember thinking that both sides of this argument seemed to have good points.

As I've grown older, I have come to realize there has to be a healthy balance between law and grace. Looking back, I see that I never really developed a living, breathing relationship with God.

Only recently did I grasp the true concept of what this means. I must have a relationship with Him in order to accept His grace. The dictionary defines *grace* as "unmerited divine assistance given humans for their regeneration or sanctification." A relationship with God (the divine assistor!) is "step one" in the life of a Christian.

But where does the law fit in to the picture? I once heard an example that really hit home. A mirror on a wall represents God's law. The mirror reflects that you have peanut butter on your face. Should you take the mirror down and scrub your face with it? No, the mirror (God's law) alerts you that you need to make a change. Are you mad at the mirror for pointing this out? No, you should be grateful. How should you handle this situation? Instead of scrubbing your face with the mirror, you need a washcloth (God's grace) to remove the peanut butter.

In the same way, the law is necessary to reflect where we need God's help and grace. His law actually frees us. God wants to make our lives pure by saying, "Here is what will hurt you: Stay away from it." And He even goes one step further. He gives you the strength to keep His law. Will you always "feel" this assistance? No, but that doesn't mean it's not there. Once you make the decision to do what's right, the windows of heaven are opened to help you go through with it. The peace that comes from being in harmony with God's will is wonderful. Our lives are to be guided by the principles of grace to show the world the benefits of *obedience* to the law.

Let's look at how Jesus lived the law. He told us in Matthew 22 to love God with all our hearts and our neighbors as ourselves. Have you ever wondered if this statement replaced the law in the Old Testament? I've certainly entertained the thought that doing what Jesus said in the above texts would be much easier to accomplish. All Christians would have to do is love God and their neighbors, and life would be peachy, right? Well, yes—sort of!

If you think about it, Jesus was just summarizing the Old Testament law. The first four commandments talk about how we, as people, can demonstrate our love for God, and the last six commandments show how we can demonstrate our love for others. Jesus lived His life for God and others. He loved and touched people in beautiful ways. John Ortberg states, "God's purpose in guidance is not to get us to perform the right actions. His purpose is to help us become the right kind of people."

So how do believing and living the law of God give me true freedom? They give me the freedom to experience life the way God intended it to be. I can have peace and contentment in following God's will. "I will delight myself in thy commandments, which I have loved" (Psalm 119:47).

1. How do you feel about the law?
2. Who was God's law intended for?
3. Is God's law set in stone, or does it vary by circumstance and situation?
4. Did Jesus change the Ten Commandments or explain them?
5. Do you need to have a relationship with God to keep the Ten Commandments?
6. Can keeping the law bring you joy?

Kellie Van Eyk, 30, lives near Raleigh, North Carolina, with her husband, John, and daughter, Brooke. She is a certified occupational therapist assistant who enjoys photography, camping, travel, and being a mom.

19

THE SABBATH

Jennifer Savatovich

Why Should I Care?

Honoring the seventh-day Sabbath through joyful celebration is a weekly reminder of the miracle of Creation and my redemption in Christ.

How Can I Know?

Exodus 31:17	Matthew 12:12
Exodus 20:8-11	Luke 6:5
Ezekiel 20:12	Leviticus 23:3
Ezekiel 20:20	Leviticus 23:32
Psalm 118:24	Genesis 2:2
Deuteronomy 5:14, 15	Exodus 16:23
Mark 2:27, 28	Exodus 23:12
Isaiah 58:13	Exodus 31:13

During spring break in eleventh grade I joined an Adventist Development and Relief Agency mission trip to Guyana. We spent two weeks in a tiny village building outhouses, teaching Vacation Bible School, and learning about the people.

Our first weekend there the neighboring village had walked 14 miles to spend Sabbath in our village, and this week it was our turn to travel. I had just finished drying the breakfast dishes when I heard a great commotion outside. The other women and I ran out of the thatched hut to see what was going on. Around the bend came the rattiest looking tractor I had ever seen in my life. It was a good 20 years old, rusting heavily, and rumbling loudly. Hitched to the back was a makeshift cart used for hauling animals, building supplies, and whatever else. I looked at my fellow missionaries in disbelief. "We're going to church in *that?*"

The entire village gathered around and began to pile onto the cart. Those who were stronger stood in the middle, while the weaker ones stood near the edges and could hang on to the sides. All in all, about 50 people had crammed themselves onto this contraption. With a whistle from the driver and a cheer from the crowd, we were off!

I expected a nice leisurely drive through the jungle. Instead, we went ripping through the trees at breakneck speed, tearing around the path as though the tractor were on fire! Every turn sent us smashing into each other.

At first I had my doubts about arriving in one piece, but as the trip wore on, the other missionaries and I grew more confident in our driver's skills. Soon we were singing and laughing with the village members, who were more accustomed to this particular form of transportation.

When we arrived at the other village, all the people were already gathered around the church, ready to greet us. As I looked around the village, what I saw stopped me dead in my tracks. The villagers were very poor; most people lived in huts, while a few had house-type structures built on stilts for the flood season. The church, however, was built with cinderblocks. Villagers had pooled their money and resources to create a more permanent building. There was only one room, empty except for a wooden pulpit in the front, and "pews" made of wood planks and cinderblocks. I also began to notice, really notice, the people around me. Not everyone was wearing shoes. The villagers were dressed in their least ragged clothes.

As I sat with the villagers and participated in the church service, I started to think about home. Would I travel 14 miles through heavy traffic in a beat-up truck with 49 other people to hear a sermon? How many times had I complained about having nothing to wear to church when I was staring at a closet full of clothes? Was I really appreciating the Sabbath as these villagers were?

Until that moment I had never realized the true value of the seventh-day Sabbath. It was just something I had grown up with, something I always did. The Sabbath had never seemed very personal to me, so I simply went through the day in a mechanical sort of way—sneaking peeks at the clock, eagerly anticipating sundown. This Sabbath in the middle of a jungle opened my eyes to the wonderful gift that God had given me.

Years and years ago God looked over the wonders of His creation. Six days were spent delighting the universe with His miraculous new planet, amazing it with His majestic power. In all His planning and wisdom, God didn't just call it quits after the sixth day and head back to heaven. He knew that Adam and Eve, and all those who followed after them, would need a special connection to Him. So He introduced the Sabbath.

The Sabbath is many blessings rolled into one. It stands as a symbol of Creation, a weekly reminder that God took time to shape our world and lovingly designed us with His own hands. The Sabbath is also a symbol of redemption. God delivered His people, the children of Israel, from slavery in Egypt. The Sabbath, already a symbol of Creation to them, became a symbol of deliverance (see Deuteronomy 5:15). Likewise, we should view the Sabbath as an escape from the daily grind. It provides time to step back from our busy lives and nurture our relationship with the God who set time aside for just that purpose. Most of all, the Sabbath is a demonstration of God's love for His people and His desire to spend special time with them. He chose a specific day, the seventh day, to make sure that everyone had the same opportunity (see Exodus 20:8-10). I used to wonder if it really mattered which day we spent in worship, but after personal study I realized that God specified the seventh day, and He hasn't changed His mind.

Being in university has heightened my appreciation of the Sabbath. Six days of attending classes, working two jobs, studying, and squeezing in some semblance of a social life has got me beat! I really look forward to sunset on Friday, when I know I can have 24 guilt-free hours away from my daily stress and spend time with God. Before, I dreaded the Sabbath because of all the activities I "couldn't" do on that day. Now, after taking time to understand the Sabbath and what it's really about, I value it for that same reason.

It was that rejection of the daily grind and the appreciation of the special day with God that I first experienced in the tiny Guyanese church. The hosting village served a delicious lunch after the church service. No one was excluded. We sat around the church on logs and stones, talking about what a wonderful day it was. That was the first time I wasn't eager for the Sabbath to be over. Here we were, sharing our experiences, discussing our frustrations, and seeking advice for our problems. There was a true sense of Christian community, a feeling of togetherness.

I could almost imagine the first Sabbath when Adam and Eve, finishing off the last bits of fresh pineapple, might have chatted with God concerning the new animals and how strange some of them looked. They could have talked about Creation, taken a stroll through the Garden of Eden, or just spent time enjoying each other's company.

When the day was over, they might have watched the sunset together with a sense of fulfillment, yet with the same sense of longing I feel thousands of years after their existence—longing for the next Sabbath to come.

"This is the day which the Lord has made; we will rejoice and be glad in it" (Psalm 118:24, NKJV).

1. Do you feel it's important to observe the Sabbath at all? Why or why not?
2. How can keeping the Sabbath benefit you?
3. What are some reasons that God created the Sabbath?
4. What kind of activities could you engage in on the Sabbath that would nurture your relationship with Christ?
5. If you already observe the Sabbath, are there activities that you participate in that you question the appropriateness of?
6. The Bible says that Jesus performed miracles and healed the sick on the Sabbath. What does that tell you about the nature of the Sabbath?

7. What do you think about the observance of Sabbath on a day other than the seventh day?

8. Is the Sabbath something that you want to make more important in your life? How do you plan to achieve this new goal?

Jennifer Savatovich, 20, divides her time between Andrews University in Michigan and her home in Newmarket, Ontario, Canada. She regrets the fact that she has never again been on a tractor ride through the jungle.

20

STEWARDSHIP
Jim Lounsbury

Why Should I Care?
As stewards of God, we have an incredible opportunity to give, considering what we have been given.

How Can I Know?

1 Chronicles 29:12-15

Job 35:8

Proverbs 11:24

Proverbs 20:5

Matthew 5:13

Matthew 5:43-48

Matthew 6:31-34

Matthew 19:19

Matthew 23:23

Matthew 25:34-40

Luke 14:12-14

Malachi 3:8-12

1 Corinthians 9:9-14

2 Corinthians 8:1-15

Romans 15:26, 27

The truck was a yellow beast—one of those vehicular demons that haunt you from the rearview mirror as you drive down the highway. The eight-cylinder engine growled beneath a rusting exterior like a wolf caught in a trap—hard to tell whether it was ready to die, or just waiting until you turned the other way. No one else in my family liked the truck.

I was proud to sit in the driver's seat. Driving was a novelty to me, a 14-year-old, and driving the Ford felt dangerous. Just as lion-taming must feel to someone behind the whip for the first time.

It was a fantastic day in western Washington. Hardly a cloud in the sky, people laughing and cuddling one another, and all those tender details you usually delve into when telling someone about a perfect afternoon.

But the truck was all I was thinking about that day. Right up to the second that my 6-year-old sister fell off her inner tube and disappeared beneath the surface of the Snoqualmie River. Adrenaline has a way of changing thought patterns.

We had been taking turns driving the truck downriver. It was a family outing, and while the rest of the family floated the one-mile stretch to the suspension bridge below, one person would drive the truck downstream to pick up the adventurers for another ride.

We must have done it a hundred times. Not that day, but in the past we had spent whole days floating down this stretch of river with no incidents.

Which is why it was strange that I stopped to watch my family float through the rapids. In the dozen or so times the truck and I had bumped and churned down the dirt road next to the river, I had driven right by the small set of rapids on the corner. But this time I decided to stop and watch. Maybe the driving was getting boring—hard to say.

I parked my backside on a rock to wait for the family to appear. I may have even left the engine running in the Ford (it was a pain to start), but I can't be sure. Finally they appeared, floating around the bend with their bathing suits and smiles on.

My mother was holding hands with my sisters, Jenny and Mary, who sat proudly on their own inner tubes. Dad was holding my younger brother, Joey, in his lap. Everyone appeared to be having a great time.

The scene was peaceful until they hit the rapids at the bend of the river. My memory of the day is a little foggy, but Mom must have nearly lost her balance, because she let go of Mary's hand. Dad was busy holding on to Joey. And Jenny was probably in her world of oblivion, enjoying the moment through her stained-glass-blue eyes.

What I do remember with accuracy was the look of terror on my mother's face. At first I misunderstood the reaction, thinking she might be losing her balance. Then I saw her looking at the empty inner tube in the middle of the river.

Mary has fallen off. The thought sank in like a dagger.

Scanning the water, I saw a small hand emerge from the rapids for a brief second. Without thinking, I jumped into the river. Swimming underwater toward the hand I had glimpsed, I moved my arms back and forth in front of me—trying to find a hand, a knee, anything.

With empty lungs and a body screaming for oxygen, I kicked forward. Finally I felt an arm. Lifting Mary over my head and out of the water, I let her take the first breath.

As I emerged from the water I could hear Mary coughing and sputtering. *She's still alive,* I thought. It was a beautiful sound.

At the side of the river I sat on the smooth rocks of a once-submerged riverbed. Mary cried softly at my side. She leaned into me and held me like a hero.

"I didn't think anyone would come," she said between sobs. "I put my hand up so you would see me, but I didn't know if you would find me."

I held back the emotion welling up in the corners of my eyes and stoically switched into big-brother mode. Tousling her hair, I laughed it off with a smile and replied, "Instead of putting your hand up, try swimming next time . . ."

It is hard to forget someone who has sincerely needed your help. Especially if you were able to provide it, free of expectations. There is a human need to give and to share what we have.

However, this need conflicts with the common social archetypes of Western society. Guard your time. Give sparingly. Manage your affairs to benefit yourself. Don't get in the habit of doing large favors for small people.

When my sister Mary disappeared beneath the rapids that day, my reaction was mechanical. Every movement was made with calculated precision, and, as a junior lifeguard, I had the necessary skills to follow through with the task.

OK. Are you ready to step through a different door? A door in which you may be held accountable? Imagine a busy street, pulsing with people. (Close your eyes for a moment if you must; then read on.)

There are people out there drowning in their own lives. Whether they are on the building site, the beach, or the street, there are people putting their hands up for help. Their eyes seem to scream, *Just listen and be interested in my life!* Often people need only a moment of your time—a demonstration that you are willing to shut up about yourself, or spend a moment laughing.

Those in need are interested in people who have their lives together. How many times have you approached an angry, lost person for help? Predictably, we look to successful people as our role models: celebrities, teachers, parents, and friends.

What do you think makes these people attractive? What makes them stand out?

Successful people manage their lives wisely. They have a good grasp of where their talents lie, and they hone those abilities. They are successful in their relationships, their jobs, and their hobbies. And they still have time to mow the lawn.

Being a well-balanced person puts your life onstage. This can be a difficult place to live, but the advantages are incredible. Imagine not only feeling satisfied with a life well lived, but knowing that others are benefiting from your friendship and that God has given you gifts to give those that you love.

In 2 Corinthians 8 Paul writes of the Macedonian churches that gave of their ability and beyond. These were ordinary people who found joy in giving of themselves. Their actions are an example of what true stewardship can be—scanning the water for hands raised in desperation. Giving when it is more human to take. Searching for ways to balance your life, so you have something to give.

Living with stewardship means living efficiently. When God is actively driving the horses of my time, the days become longer and the stress becomes bearable. Somehow I find a balance in the spiritual, physical, and social areas of my life, and I have more time for those that I love.

Living in a Web-based, interactive, pro-choice, 28-hour day, flat-management-style world, it can be difficult to slow down. It often seems more efficient to point your head in one direction and forget about everything else until you reach your goals.

But success is built on moderation and perseverance. Happiness comes from sharing the journey. Satisfaction comes from reaching goals together.

People need people who have their life together. Somewhere people are drowning. Are you willing to jump in? If you can live a balanced life, with stewardship as a priority, you may just be able to drown somebody in whatever it is that they need.

1. What time is it? How much time can you schedule for someone else today?
2. Do people ever call you to ask for help? If not, why?
3. How much time do you spend taking care of your own needs each day?
4. What is something you are exceptional at doing?
5. Do you keep a daily schedule?
6. Has anyone truly affected you in your life? How do they handle their time?
7. When do you feel most able to give of yourself?

Jim Lounsbury, 24, has red hair and still calls Seattle home. He is a registered nurse who spent most of his time at Southern Adventist University trying to fit in as an English major. Now he runs a small production company in Newcastle, Australia (www.salt.net.au), committed to producing Christian theater and film. His hobbies include writing, photography, travel, and backpacking. Jim is married to Lynette, who chose to retain her maiden name, Roberts, because Lynette Lounsbury is too alliterative. (Now, that's an English major.)

21

CHRISTIAN BEHAVIOR

Brian Reed

Why Should I Care?

My behavior is a response to Jesus' love and acceptance of me.

How Can I Know?

Romans 1:4, 5

Romans 2:4, 11

Romans 3:20

Romans 3:23-26

Romans 5:5-11

Romans 6:1-5

Romans 8:1

Romans 12:1, 2

2 Corinthians 5:14, 17, 20

Galatians 2:20

Galatians 5:16-26

Ephesians 4:22-24

Ephesians 4:31, 32

2 Timothy 2:22-26

James 1:22-25

Matthew 25:34-40

There she was again, standing at my bedroom door. "Did you read your Bible and pray today?"

"No, Mother, I haven't."

It seemed as though she would never stop asking. Why did it matter, anyway? I had read through the whole Bible already, and it had been one long, boring accomplishment. *Besides,* I thought, *I'm reading this Louis L'Amour Western, a fine analysis of early American culture. I can't stop now—the hero's about to shoot the bad guys and then get the girl!*

Five years later, as I began my college career, reading the Bible and praying was still very low on my priority list. Social life came first, followed by sports, with studies dragging along behind. My relationship with God consisted of Bible class, required dorm worships, and church on Sabbath. To me religion was rules: do not swear, do not dance, do not attend movies, do not drink, do not smoke, do not have premarital sex, do attend required worships, do go to church, do read your Bible, and do pray. My faith was based on a set of requirements and not on a saving God who was reaching out in love to me. Unable to distinguish between the two, I gave up on both.

I was so discouraged. A friend told me to "give it all to Jesus," and I laughed at him openly. The idea of giving it all to Jesus seemed like a joke to me. I knew Jesus: He was the guy who made all the rules. He was the one who had imposed all the restrictions on me my whole life. Why would I want anything to do with Him? I decided God didn't exist, because it seemed easier than believing in Him. I became a slave to marijuana and alcohol, and slowly I slipped into the deepest depression of my life.

One day while sitting in my dorm room trying to study, I heard my mother's voice in my thoughts. *Did you read your Bible and pray today?*

I wanted to laugh and scream out, "No way!" but instead I felt a strange sadness. How could I read my Bible and pray? Who would I be praying to?

Then I did laugh. I *could* read my Bible and pray—just to prove to myself and my mother that God didn't exist!

So I prayed: "Uh, hello? If You're out there listening, prove it, because my life stinks, and I'm not happy." Reaching over, I grabbed the Bible off the bookshelf and opened it up to Matthew.

As I read the Bible I began to understand the story of a Man who loved people who were the worst of sinners. I discovered a Man who loved prostitutes, tax collectors, Zealots, Roman soldiers, and even legalistic Pharisees. The stories in the Bible showed me that when people met Jesus face to face, they wanted to change. When they met Him face to face they wanted to live right lives for Him—not because He imposed rules on them, but because they knew He loved and accepted them as they were. I noticed that even the disciples who hung out with Him all the time had struggles. Most of them denied Him at His crucifixion, and one even hanged himself. These weren't picture-perfect Christians. However, Jesus didn't focus on their behavior; He told them about love, forgiveness, and His kingdom. He befriended them first, and He taught them not to judge each other. I figured that hanging out with a Guy like that would be pretty cool.

So I did.

And I lived happily ever after! Well, not exactly. I was still smoking pot and drinking. But as the next two years of college passed by and came to a close, I found myself praying and reading more and more, and smoking and drinking less and less. The closer I got to Jesus, the less desire or need I had for the harmful behaviors in my life. Eventually, as my relationship with Jesus grew, I had to make decisions about my behavior. I discovered that being best friends with Jesus could be quite confronting at times. I had to start choosing Him over a lot of other things that had been important to me. It wasn't always easy, and I often fell back into my old ways, but Jesus' love and acceptance always won me back.

Fast-forward three years to the present. Everything is picture-perfect, right? Wrong. I still struggle. But my struggles are different. Most of them exist in my mind. However, Jesus has made a remarkable difference, and I know that He is right here inside my heart struggling along with me. Do I behave as a perfect Christian should? No, I don't, but because of Jesus' love and acceptance of me, I choose to try my hardest to do the things He would have me do. I also try my hardest *not* to do things that will damage my relationship with Him. I know when I fall down He will be there to pick me up. Jesus has led me and is leading me into the right kind of behavior, and I trust Him.

"Did you read your Bible and pray today?" There's that voice in my thoughts again.

"Yes, Mother, I did, and I will tomorrow and the day after and for the rest of my life! Thanks for asking, though. How about you?"

1. Do you ever feel discouraged by your mistakes? Do you feel as though God doesn't love you after you make a mistake?

2. What is God's response to you when you fall into sin?

3. What comes first—right living or a right relationship with Jesus? Why?

4. How does your behavior reflect your relationship with Jesus?

5. If we are saved by grace, does that mean we can do whatever we want?

6. When you choose to do something you know is wrong, is it God who turns His back on you, or is it you who turn your back on God?

7. Why is it so hard to pray after we choose to do something we know will harm our relationship with Jesus?

Brian Reed, 27, has just finished a year in Melbourne, Australia, as a volunteer youth pastor. He is currently a teacher at Cascade Christian Academy in Wenatchee, Washington.

22

MARRIAGE AND THE FAMILY

Christina Anderson (with Bernie Anderson)

Why Should I Care?

God created the family to be a safe place for growth, both physically and spiritually.

How Can I Know?

Isaiah 41:7

Deuteronomy 10:20

Genesis 2:23, 24

1 Corinthians 11:18

Genesis 1:31

Genesis 2:20

Malachi 2:14

Ephesians 5:21-33

Matthew 19:6

Genesis 4:1

Proverbs 5:18

Hebrews 13:4

John 13:1

1 Corinthians 13:4-8

Genesis 1:26, 2:15

Genesis 1:28

Ephesians 5:23-28

1 Peter 3:1-8

Finally, after three long months of waiting and wanting, we moved into our first home in Arlington, Texas. We had promised each other that after seminary we would buy a home for our children. And God had provided a wonderful home just right for our needs. Our daughters, Madison and Brooklyn, each had their own room, and Bernie had an office. God had truly blessed.

We stayed up all night that first day, unpacking and discovering things that we had forgotten we owned. Madison literally dumped out every box of toys that she could find. It was like Christmas in March. Two weeks later, after days of nonstop work, we had our home just the way we wanted it. It was a wonderful feeling.

If you have ever been in Texas during the spring season, you know that "severe weather" is the norm. But since I (Christina) am from Arizona, I panic every time the word "tornado" is uttered. It takes a while to get adjusted to the tornado warnings flashing across the TV screen!

One evening as we drove toward home, Bernie realized that this could possibly be a bad night: The sky quickly grew darker, and an eerie feeling hung in the air. The radio confirmed our fears and indicated that a tornado had touched down just to the north of us. We quickly came into the house and turned on the news. What a blessing—the tornado was heading away from us! Since it seemed that we were in the clear, we sat down to dinner with a sense of relief.

But just as we started to eat, the electricity blinked a couple times and eventually went out. It was completely dark in our home. The girls fussed as Bernie rounded up the flashlights. But since we knew that the storm was heading away from us, we continued to listen to the rain without worrying about the strong gusts of wind outside the door.

About halfway through dinner we heard a bang at the door. Bernie opened it to the relief of our friends, who just *knew* that our new home had been destroyed by the tornado.

We were completely bewildered. "We thought the tornado was in another city!" Bernie explained

And then we looked out our front door.

Our neighbor's tree lay toppled in their front yard, only inches from the kitchen window. Glancing down the block, we began to see why our friends were scared: lights flashed and sirens wailed everywhere. It was a frightening feeling—only three blocks from our home the neighborhood was full of destruction and chaos. The tornado had hit with a vengeance. We put the girls into the stroller and began walking down the streets.

The power that wind can have in the form of a tornado is amazing. Homes were destroyed, utility poles snapped in half, cars overturned and lying in yards, and fence pieces strewn everywhere. People milled around, stunned, looking at the heaps of wood that used to be their homes. It was the closest thing to a war zone that I had ever seen. Utter destruction is the only way that I know to describe it.

As we walked through the rubble, we realized just how fortunate we had been. Bernie walked us home and then went back to see what could be done for the families who had lost almost everything. He talked with the agency involved in providing assistance to those in need. He made sure that they had a place to sleep and offered them a word of comfort. He offered to open our church, to provide transportation and a warm meal. Although most arrangements had already been made, he wanted neighbors to know that we cared for them when they needed it most. When Bernie returned, our family had a time of prayer. We praised God for His protection, and we asked for Him to draw close to those who were not as fortunate.

Afterward we kept saying, "Not a single toy was turned over in our backyard . . . how could that be?" It can only be described as a *God thing*. While the storm wreaked havoc in our own neighborhood, we felt safe and secure in our home.

After this experience it became very clear to us that families can be devastated by storms. Not just tornadoes or hurricanes, but the storms of life: the "unseen storm." More than anything else, Satan wants to destroy the happiness and security that can exist in families. His tactics are ruthless: He plots and schemes because he knows that he has but a short time left before Jesus comes.

Bernie and I see marriage and the family as God's special gift to humanity. In the context of a loving marriage, there is tremendous safety. That was God's design from the beginning. First, He made a home for us, next He created us, and then He created marriage and family for our enjoyment. When a man and woman come together to begin the journey of marriage, they make a solemn and sanctified commitment that they will create for each other a safe haven. A place where husband and wife can freely share their dreams, desires, and their deepest secrets. When this type of true intimacy is achieved, then the relationship is as God intended. It will withstand the storms of life.

This safety also extends to the children. Children need a model of Christlike behavior. They need to know that in their family, Christ is first without exception. They need a family that lovingly guides them through childhood and into adulthood, teaching them the values that they need to maintain a Christian walk. When this type of love is demonstrated and taught, the home is a safe place for the child and the parents.

After the fall into sin God indicated that there would be "enmity" between the seed of the woman and the seed of the serpent (Genesis 3:15). The Bible also says that Satan goes about as a "roaring lion, . . . seeking whom he may devour" (1 Peter 5:8). This hatred is manifest through Satan's attacks on the family. The Bible has prophesied that ultimately the offspring of the woman would crush the serpent's head, a promise fulfilled in Christ's victory over Satan. We believe that this is a victory in which all believers and all families can share.

I look forward to gathering safely in heaven with my family and inviting Jesus over for a meal, with no more worries about storms of any kind.

1. How can you make your home a safe place for your family?
2. What role does Christ have in your marriage (family)?
3. What role does prayer have in your marriage (family)?
4. Do you agree that marriage is truly a gift from God?
5. What steps can you take to achieve a deeper level of intimacy with your spouse?
6. Does your family know how deep your level of commitment is to them and to God?
7. What is your family doing to demonstrate God's love to those around you?

Bernie and Christina live in Arlington, Texas. Bernie, 29, is an associate pastor at the Arlington, Texas, Seventh-day Adventist Church. Christina, 26, is a stay-at-home mom who leads a mom's Bible study group from home and pursues a social work degree from the University of Texas at Arlington. Bernie and Christina have two little girls: 3-year-old Madison and 9-month-old Brooklyn.

23

CHRIST'S MINISTRY IN THE HEAVENLY SANCTUARY

Teresa L. Caine

Why Should I Care?

The Bible tells us that there is a sanctuary in heaven where Christ ministers as our great high priest, making available to believers the benefits of His atoning sacrifice and performing the work of investigative judgment.

How Can I Know?

Hebrews 8:1, 2, 5; 9:11

Revelation 8:3

1 John 2:1

Revelation 20:12

1 John 1:9

2 Corinthians 5:18, 19, 21

Romans 3:24

Revelation 3:4, 5

Isaiah 43:25

Revelation 14:6, 7

Revelation 4:1-11

Revelation 5:8-14

Zechariah 3:2

1 Chronicles 13, 14

Exodus 32:33

Acts 17:30, 31

1 Corinthians 6:9, 10

November 1834

've heard that You are coming back soon, Jesus, and that we must confess our sins to be right with You." Twelve-year-old Amy Jenkins, dressed in her nightcap and gown, knelt beside her small trundle bed. Cold night air blew threw the cracks of her loft window, but she stayed warm from the fire burning in the fireplace below.

"I was wondering if You would please forgive me for shoving Sarah at school yesterday, even though she called me poor and ugly. Help me to be the kind of girl I need to be to go to heaven with You." Amy paused and thought for a minute, then continued. "Please help Sarah to be good too. And if it's not too much trouble, would You also please send rain for our crops so Daddy won't be so mad and upset all the time? Thank You, Jesus. Amen." Amy snuggled under her bed quilts and closed her eyes.

An unseen angel at Amy's side had recorded her every word. He flew swiftly to heaven to deliver Amy's prayer. In the holy place of the heavenly sanctuary Amy's prayer was added to the others' prayers.

A golden lampstand with seven torches illuminated a golden altar where Jesus was receiving the prayers and interceding as high priest on humanity's behalf. An angel holding a golden censer full of incense stood near to Him at the golden altar. To this angel was given much incense that he should offer it with all the prayers upon the golden altar.

Behind the altar hung a shimmering veil that separated the holy compartment from the Most Holy compartment. In the Most Holy Place the Father sat upon His throne, where He was being reconciled to every penitent sinner through Jesus.

Amy's prayer rose with the incense as a sweet fragrance, and Christ added His intercession on Amy's behalf. "Father, I plead forgiveness for My repentant child Amy. May My blood sacrificed for her be an acceptable substitute in her place, and may her sins be blotted out. May she be restored as a joint heir to My kingdom."

Behind the shimmering veil the Father heard. Christ's own righteousness was given to her, and the name Amy Jenkins was recorded upon the sacred pages of the book of life. From His priestly throne Jesus looked down from heaven and lovingly smiled at the sleeping Amy, who was unaware that a gentle rain fell outside her tiny log cabin home.

Spring 1844

Like lightning an angel flashed through midheaven shouting to every nation, tribe, tongue, and people on earth: "Fear God and give him glory, because the hour of his judgment has come" (Rev. 14:7, NIV). While no earthly ear heard the actual voice of the angel messenger, many Christians across distant lands had read the angel's message in Scripture. There was a great religious awakening as they spread the words of warning from Daniel and Revelation that foretold the end of prophetic time and of the great event that was about to take place in heaven.

October 22, 1844

Gabriel flew into the holy place to meet Jesus at the golden altar. His large wings folded humbly about his shining torso as he bowed before the King of kings. "The warning of judgment has been sounded throughout the earth, my Lord. The temple is open. The thrones have been set in place for the elders, and all the heavenly host are in attendance. Your Father awaits You now, my Lord."

"The time of the end is at hand, Gabriel," said Jesus. "My sacrifice to save humanity has been made complete. Today, the last of all time prophecies is fulfilled with the beginning of this investigative judgment. It won't be long now till I can bring My faithful children home."

There was a distant glimmer in Jesus' eyes as He looked again upon the earth. His brilliant countenance showed a mix of fondness and sorrow. A long, quiet moment passed before He turned His gaze back to His beloved chief angel and declared, "Let the judgment time begin."

A brilliant cloud as bright as the noonday sun began to swirl under Jesus' feet and billowed out all around Him. It lifted Him up and carried Him beyond the shimmering veil into the Most Holy Place.

The Father, the Ancient of Days, was seated upon His throne there. His vesture was like snow and His hair like pure wool. Thousands upon thousands of angels attended Him. The appearance of His throne was like that of a jasper stone, a blackish-green crystal, and there was an emerald-like rainbow encircling it. The Father's throne was ablaze with flames, its wheels a burning fire, and a river of fire flowed out before

Him. Flashes of lightning and peals of thunder also proceeded from His awesome majesty. Twenty-four other thrones were set up there in the Most Holy Place, and upon them sat 24 elders clothed in white garments and wearing golden crowns upon their heads. They fell down before the Father to worship Him and cast their crowns before Him.

As Jesus appeared through the veil, the angels, elders, and all the heavenly host shouted with a loud voice, "Worthy is the Lamb who was slain to receive power and riches and wisdom, and strength and honor and glory and blessing!" (Revelation 5:12, NKJV).

As the bright, swirling cloud carried Jesus across the sea of crystal glass that expanded between Him and His Father, Jesus' eyes fell upon the ark of the covenant containing God's precious laws. It had been opened for the judgment. There also was the book of life, and lying next to it were the books of record, each opened to reveal where angels had recorded every human deed. All was set to investigate humanity and to judge those who were righteous by the acceptance of Christ's sacrifice made in their behalf.

As Jesus approached His Father, the elders fell down and worshiped Him. Each elder played a golden harp and sang a new song: "You are worthy to take the scroll and to open its seals, because you were slain, and with your blood you purchased men for God from every tribe and language and people and nation. You have made them to be a kingdom and priests to serve our God; and they will reign on the earth" (verses 9, 10, NIV).

Jesus took His seat and began with the first names written in the book of life: Adam and Eve.

"They are not worthy of Your salvation!" shouted an angry voice from earth below. Satan had been watching the heavenly procession with hatred in his soul and now stood ready to accuse all those whom Jesus named His own. "They lost their purity when they sinned against You, Jesus! They are no longer fit to live in Your supposed perfect little kingdom!"

"They repented of all their sins, Satan," Jesus calmly replied, "and they have been forgiven."

"That's not good enough!" Satan retorted. "They lost their rights to heaven and to this world when they gave up their allegiance to You by succumbing to me. They and this world rightly belong to me!"

"I have bought everything back with the blood of My sacrifice." Jesus revealed His nail-pierced hands as a reminder of the price He paid to redeem lost humanity. Holding His arms up before the Father and the holy angels, Jesus declared, "I know them by name. Because of their choice to return their love and allegiance to me, I have graven them on the palms of My hands" (see Isaiah 49:16).

To Satan He said, "The Lord rebuke thee, O Satan. 'Is not this a brand plucked out of the fire?' [Zechariah 3:2]. They shall walk with Me in white, for they are worthy."

The judgment continued as names throughout all of history were brought up for investigation. Satan never let up on his evil allegations as he accused the brethren day and night. For righteous souls redeemed by Christ, pardon was entered against their names in the books of record, and their sins were blotted out. Their names remained recorded in the book of life, and their eternal salvation was secured.

Some souls in history, however, were lost to Satan's allegations.

"Now, You know You can't claim Saul! He tried to make it without You and found out how impossible it was," taunted Satan. Jesus noted the unrepented and unforgiven sins remaining upon the books of record belonging to Saul. "He consulted an evil spirit and would not trust Me," Jesus sadly declared. In great sorrow He blotted out Saul's name from the book of life, recorded when he had once been a faithful follower of God.

Any Day Now

The years have rolled by, and the investigative judgment in heaven has completed its inquiry into the dead. Now the focus of heaven is turned to the judgment of the living on earth.

"He's mine!" Satan hissed as he danced around Danny Callaway, a young college student wounded in a fatal car accident that had just occurred.

"He has not completed his choice yet, Satan," replied Jesus. An extra angel was immediately dispatched to the young man's side as he lay barely conscious on the hospital gurney.

"Danny, can you hear me?" asked Pastor James. Danny's minister had been called to respond to Danny's crisis.

"Yeah." Danny replied weakly. His breathing was labored from the lung injuries. "Ricky and Joe didn't make it, did they?"

"No, son. I'm sorry."

The tears rolled from Danny's bloodshot eyes. "And the family that was in the other car? I remember hearing one of the kids crying as we were being pulled out of the wreckage."

"It was a terrible accident, Danny. You are the only one who survived it."

Danny sobbed in spite of the tremendous pain it brought to his internal injuries. *You killed them all!* Satan whispered into Danny's ear. *It's all your fault. Your friends told you that you were too drunk to drive, but you wouldn't listen. Had to be the big shot.*

"It's all my fault." Danny tried to regain a little composure so he could talk. "I had too much to drink. I've tried to quit drinking, but I can't. I don't deserve to live."

"You are not hopeless, Danny. No matter how tough it is, God is tougher. He can help you."

Jesus has the power to help you overcome, Danny. The unseen angel stroked Danny's head and tried to comfort his restless soul.

You don't deserve Jesus, chided Satan. *Remember the money you stole from your mother this afternoon just so you could go buy your liquor?*

"God doesn't love me. Look at me. I don't even love me."

"No matter how bad things get, Danny, Jesus never stops loving you," said Pastor James. "He died on that cross for you. He died for this very moment to save you."

Trust Him, whispered the Holy Spirit into Danny's conscience. *Accept Him now before it's too late.*

"All you have to do is accept His forgiveness and take His love into your heart right now." Pastor James took Danny's hand into his.

Oh, yeah? What is Ricky's family going to think about you now? And Joe's? Satan pressed the guilt home. *They will never forgive you. How will you ever face your friends again? And what about the law? They are going to charge you with manslaughter for drinking and driv-*

ing! How's God going to help you out of all that?

Trust Him, pleaded the Holy Spirit. *God is strong, and He loves you. Trust Him now.*

"No," Danny sobbed again as he took his hand back from Pastor James. "I can't live with myself, knowing what I did to my best friends and the kids of that family."

Danny began gasping for air. His injured lungs had collapsed. Emergency measures were taken, but Danny slipped away into death.

Satan was exultant, but tears rolled from Jesus' eyes as He blotted out Danny's name from the book of life.

Very Soon

The investigative judgment has ended. Every living soul has been judged. Christ's ministry in the heavenly sanctuary is complete. With a thundering voice Jesus rises and proclaims, "Let the righteous remain righteous and the unrighteous remain unrighteous still" (see Revelation 22:11).

With that He removes His priestly attire and is draped in His royal robes and crown. The thunderclouds roll as Jesus prepares to make His second appearance—to bring His righteous children home.

1. Why do you think the Bible refers to Jesus as our high priest?
2. How would you describe the investigative judgment to a friend?
3. Why would a loving God judge humanity at all?
4. Why is Jesus able to claim saved sinners as His own?
5. How do you feel about the judgment of God?
6. What would you tell a friend who was fearful of God's judgment?

Teresa Caine is 43 years young and the mother of five. She and her husband live in Cleveland, Tennessee. She enjoys hiking, camping, photography, and writing and speaking about social issues (especially those affecting the church).

24

THE SECOND COMING

Sarah Coleman Kelnhofer

Why Should I Care?

Believing in the second coming of Christ provides me with hope for a better future and the incentive to live a better present.

How Can I Know?

John 14:1-4	Matthew 16:26, 27
Psalm 50:3-6	1 Thessalonians 5:2-6
Matthew 24:23-31, 36-51	Matthew 25:31-46
Isaiah 25:9	Philippians 2:5-11
Hosea 10:12	Luke 21:25-28
1 Thessalonians 4:16-18	2 Peter 3:11-13
Titus 2:11-14	Matthew 7:21
Hebrews 10:27, 28	2 Timothy 4:8
Acts 1:11	2 Corinthians 5:10
Job 19:25	Revelation 22:12-21
Revelation 1:7	Matthew 24:14

During the first months of our marriage my husband and I lived in Indiana and often braved city traffic to visit the metropolis of Chicago. One trip in particular stays fresh in my mind.

The drive had been uneventful except for the usual discussions about the temperature of the car and the volume of the radio. Uneventful, that is, until Chris insisted on listening to several talk-radio programs in a row. I soon tired of the monotony and politely offered to change the station. Chris refused to budge.

Fine, I thought. *I'm tuning out.* I crossed my arms and stared out the window, hoping in vain that he'd get the hint. Inwardly I fumed. *How could he ignore my wishes?* My thoughts awhirl, I barely noticed the passing scenery.

But as my frustration cooled, I began focusing on the view above me. First I counted telephone poles, marveling at the amount of wire needed to connect every household to a dial tone. Then I noticed the sky behind the wires. In keeping with Indiana's stormy reputation, a high sheaf of clouds blotted out the sun. *Not surprising,* I sniffed. *The day's always rotten when Chris and I argue.* I continued studying those bland winter clouds, watching their noiseless rush across the heavens until one odd shape caught my attention.

The cloud was surprisingly dark, at least three shades darker than the clouds behind it. A small, silent outcast, it hovered somewhere between the earth and its overcast backdrop. I watched, transfixed, as the ceiling above it shifted and swayed while this lonely sentinel remained steady. I forgot about Chris. The drone of the radio faded away. The car, the traffic, the wires, the asphalt—they all disappeared. I watched and waited.

And then it happened. Sunlight, so long hidden behind those impenetrable clouds, shoved its way toward earth. It flowed through the atmosphere and came to rest behind the object of my scrutiny.

The black cloud suddenly came to life. Lit from within, its sharp edges became unbearably bright as it inched closer to earth—closer to me. I couldn't look away. One haunting question washed through my mind: Was this the cloud of Jesus' second coming? The familiar belief that He would arrive in a cloud, initially "as small as a man's hand" (1 Kings 18:44, NIV), echoed through my brain.

It can't be! my logic protested. *There's been no warning, no chance for repentance! And boy, do I need to repent!*

I squinted at the cloud. If this really were the Son of man, it wouldn't matter if I apologized to Chris or not. My fate—heaven-bound or not—would already be sealed.

My present surroundings came rushing into my consciousness, and the metal walls of the car seemed suddenly fragile. Would they melt in the face of an angry God? Worse, would *I* melt as well?

My thoughts began traveling in several directions at once. I remembered my childhood—the gut-wrenching fear that Jesus would appear in the midst of each new thunderstorm. A thousand sermons flicked through my mind, "amen"-filled lectures foretelling the Saviour's return. I visualized the moment of His arrival—pure white and as blindingly brilliant as the edges of that swelling black cloud. My own meager life—filled with self, self, and more self—would be the one dark smudge on the glory of that moment. Would my family miss me? Would Chris leave earth without me? My breath came short and quick.

And still the cloud grew.

"Sarah, do you have to go to the bathroom?" Chris's voice slit into my thoughts like a razor, and I flinched.

"Huh?" My eyes never left the cloud. How could I tell him what was about to happen? He'd see soon enough.

"There's a rest stop ahead." Chris yawned. "Wanna take a break?"

The world of necessities won. I glanced ahead to the blue sign with the arrow. "Sure."

Quickly, guiltily, I turned to the window again. *The cloud had disappeared!* Now a thinning strand of vapor, it looked as unobtrusive as the rest of the midwinter sky. I blinked. *Could it be?* The sound of the radio returned, and I remembered my frustration with Chris. Dry heater air blasted me in the face. Telephone wires, telephone poles, and an occasional tree flew past my window. For now, at least, the earth was safe.

"Chris." I had to say it. "I'm sorry I got upset about the radio . . ."

I wish these Second Coming scares were infrequent occurrences, but they're not. They usually coincide quite nicely with my bad moods. Perhaps it is just my imagination, but after this has happened several times, I've begun to think that Someone wants to get my attention.

This Someone has been planning a special event for me for thousands of years. He waited over the millennia for me to be born. He clapped His hands with pleasure when I first learned He'd be back. And He's watched my heart and my actions intensely, hoping like everything that I'll want to see Him when He comes.

And for the most part, I *do* want to see Him. I've been blessed to grow up in a Christian home with parents who mention His return with joyful anticipation. As I've found a deeper relationship with my Creator, I've been caught up in the excitement that surrounds this future event.

But some days I'm caught up in the world instead. When I'm happy I forget that there's a better alternative to this imperfect joy. When I'm sad His coming looks like a skinny carrot held up to tempt a plodding donkey forward. And when I'm angry I'd just as soon forget the future exists.

Jesus anticipated this assortment of emotions and promised to stand by me through them all. "And surely I am with you always, to the very end of the age" (Matthew 28:20, NIV). Comforting, yes. But what should I do while I wait for the "end of the age"?

Jesus presents the answer in Matthew 24, a chapter devoted entirely to the events of the future. "Who then," He asks, "is the faithful and wise servant, whom the master has put in charge of the servants of his household to give them their food at the proper time?" (verse 45, NIV).

On impulse I want to raise my hand. That's me! I'm a Christian. I've been given the responsibility to "feed" my fellow humans the bread of life until the real Source returns.

Jesus continues, "It will be good for that servant whose master finds him doing so when he returns" (verse 46, NIV).

Pretty simple, right? I should be reaching out to others, constantly offering the bread and the water that will make them "never hunger" (John 6:35) and "never thirst" again (John 4:14). Jesus goes on to describe the consequences of being unfaithful and the rewards He has planned for His *real* followers. But nowhere in this chapter does He cater to the flyaway feelings a "wise servant" might encounter as she waits for her Master's return. Why this silence?

Surely the Lord wants me to anticipate His coming. Verses such as Titus 2:13 make that clear. But here I find no pat on the shoulder, no Kleenex for my tears, no hype about the glories of the kingdom. Only a straight admonition: Be faithful. Be wise. Keep on with the work.

Perhaps this is because 2,000 years ago Jesus knew my heart. He knew the heart of each struggling servant on earth. And He knew, better than anyone else in the universe, that a serving servant is a faithful one. Perhaps if I'd been more intent on "keeping on with the work," I would have been less shaken by that mysterious cloud. Maybe I wouldn't have seen it at all. Whatever the case, I've come to the conclusion that I *am* excited about Jesus' soon return—He wants me to be. But rather than waiting with folded and trembling hands, I'm going to get busy. I'm going to use these hands to bring nourishment into a world starving for spiritual food.

Someday Jesus will return. I'll be hoping for it, praying for it, every day. And when He does—when He asks that crucial question, "Where are My faithful followers?"—I want to look up from my work, wipe my sweaty hands, and raise them both in the air. As any good servant would do.

1. How do you feel about the second coming of Jesus?

2. Are you able to tell others about His soon return?

3. Why do you think every human will see Jesus when He returns?

4. Would a "secret rapture" be out of keeping with the character of God? Why or why not?

5. How can you prepare for Jesus' second coming?

6. What would you tell someone who felt afraid or unready for the Second Coming?

7. What would you tell someone who felt content with life on this earth and had no desire for Jesus to come again? How can you cultivate a stronger desire for His return in your own life?

8. What specific work do you think Jesus wants you to do in order to be a faithful servant to Him?

Sarah Coleman Kelnhofer, 23, lives near Albuquerque, New Mexico, with her astounding husband, Chris, and several small cacti. She enjoys camping in any mountain wilderness she can find, and actually writes because she loves to. She still avoids excessive talk radio.

25

DEATH AND RESURRECTION
Nathan Brown

Why Should I Care?
In the midst of the inevitable tragedies of life, the promise of resurrection provides a glorious hope.

How Can I Know?

James 4:14	Psalm 73:24-26
Psalm 78:39	Isaiah 26:19
Job 14:1, 2	Matthew 28:1-10
Genesis 2:7, 16, 17	Mark 16:1-14
Ecclesiastes 9:5, 6, 10	Luke 24:1-12; 36-49
Psalm 146:3, 4	John 20:14-18
Romans 5:12	1 Corinthians 15
Romans 6:23	1 Thessalonians 4:15-18
2 Timothy 1:10	John 11:21-27
John 5:28, 29	Revelation 1:17, 18
Job 19:25-29	

It was a Friday morning, and I had been doing the 9:00 to 12:00 morning shift on our city's Christian radio station for just a couple weeks. As I sat in the small downtown studio overlooking the river, it was difficult to develop enthusiasm for the usual routine of station IDs and time calls. The morning slowly crept by, and I knew I needed to say "it" before my on-air shift came to an end. I felt it was something I had to do, but being new to the station, the need to check it with the station manager allowed me to put it off until after 11:00.

The terrible information had come to me in the impersonal form of an e-mail. I had checked my e-mail messages after arriving home and found a message whose subject line read "Bad news." That did not prepare me for the news contained therein. It stated simply that a friend and church pastor had died suddenly that night. He had collapsed at home and died within an hour. I was stunned.

As he had been a leader in our church, I felt I should say something in the course of my program that Friday morning. But it just did not seem right. I felt that I must have received the wrong information and that, if I did say something, someone would soon ring the station to correct such a crazy suggestion.

Somehow, by broadcasting the tragic news, it seemed it would become more real. It was almost as if I would then bear responsibility for part of the sorrow.

A little after 11:00 the station manager opened the door of the studio to say hi and see how I was doing. The story spilled out, and he supported the idea of sharing the news over the air. Now I was committed to doing it.

I had two songs to go until the next talk break. For the twentieth time that morning, I rehearsed what I would say. One song to go. I cued the final song.

My voice sounded strained as I briefly related the tragic news and asked for the prayers of the Christian community for his family and our church. I forgot much of what I had rehearsed, and soon the moment passed. As the next song played, I muted the studio microphone and looked along the river to the distant horizon, where the ocean met the sky. Filling those two minutes of radio was one of the hardest things I have ever done.

✦ ✦ ✦

As we progress through life, the reaction to death becomes an all-too-familiar feeling. The kick in the stomach when the message arrives; the nausea and confusion; the stunned hours of silently shaking one's head; the tentative reaching out to others, sharing in subdued conversations the shock and the bittersweet memories; the gradual slide into the realization of the tragedy; and the residual dull ache about which we cannot say or do anything. Through tragic repetition, this experience with death may almost come to be considered a part of life—but we can never quite accept it.

In a short story I read recently, Jorge Luis Borges describes a city so horrible that, though hidden in the midst of a vast desert, it has an influence on the rest of the world. By its mere existence, it "contaminates the past and the future and in some way even jeopardizes the stars. As long as it lasts, no one in the world can be strong or happy" (*Labyrinths,* p. 141).

Death seems to operate in a similar way in our world. As long as death remains in our world, our world will be incomplete. It is this incompleteness that jars us so violently when confronted with the appalling tragedy of death. There is something inside us that is repulsed by the apparent finality death presents.

Every funeral I have attended has been occasioned by a premature and tragic death. While any death is a tragedy, the circumstances in which deaths often occur add weight to the horror. The fragility of life is brought into contrast with the ugly brutality of death. For those who remain, there are the inevitable questions in an attempt to make sense of the senseless . . . and even now I am trying to express the inexpressible.

Yet in the midst of the sorrow, we begin to move on. It is not a choice that life must go on; it is the simple reality that life continues. However, there comes a point of searing heartbreak where one has to turn and walk away from that new graveside.

Without meaning any offense to the well-intentioned people who echo the questions from the Bible such as "O death, where is thy sting? O grave, where is thy victory?" (1 Corinthians 15:55), I often feel the need to suggest to them simply to look around at the hurt and grief that is so obvious. When I am most honest, a song played at a funeral I attended last year seems most real. The chorus includes the line: "And it feels like heaven's so far away" (The Offspring, "Gone Away").

Fortunately, we have a hope—a reality—beyond our feelings. I am cynical enough not to have to search for an explanation for the evil manifested in such tragedies. I am prepared to accept that we are in a bad place where bad things happen. But I still hope. I know there is an answer. Jesus wept, and I believe He still weeps with us—but He is also the First and the Last. He is the Living One who was dead but is now alive forever and ever. He holds the keys of death and the grave (adapted from Revelation 1:17, 18).

I think I would like to rewrite the last verse of "Abide With Me." Rather than "Where is death's sting? Where, grave, thy victory?" I would write it something like "Death still has an awful sting, and the grave seems so horribly triumphant, but I triumph still if Thou abide with me!"

As George MacDonald once wrote: "Despair dies into infinite hope." For a Christian, death is not the end of the story. The end of the story is a happy one, in the style of the best fairy tale—but it is true. The Bible—and the New Testament in particular—is filled with the hope of resurrection.

In the face of our most bitter tragedies God is still God. He loves us eternally and infinitely. No matter what our circumstances, the hope remains.

1. Why is death so jarring to us?
2. Can we ever be prepared to die? Why or why not?
3. How has God helped you, your family, or friends in a time of crisis?
4. Is it wrong for a Christian to grieve? Why or why not?
5. Think of ways you could help someone who is grieving.
6. What are the practical effects of believing death is like sleep (see Ecclesiastes 9:5, 6, 10; Luke 8:52-55; John 11:11-14), rather than one's soul living on?
7. How does the fact of Jesus' resurrection affect the way you view death?
8. What does Jesus' statement "I am the Resurrection" mean (John 11:25)?

9. Why is the hope of resurrection so important in the New Testament?

10. Think of someone you would like to meet at the resurrection. Why?

Nathan Brown, 26, lives in Townsville, Queensland, Australia. He reads (postgraduate study in literature), writes (freelance writing), delivers pizzas, and is an amateur radio DJ.

26

THE MILLENNIUM AND THE END OF SIN
Tompaul Wheeler

Why Should I Care?

This belief points to a resolution of both sin and the many questions sin brings.

How Can I Know?

Daniel 2:44

Malachi 4:1

Matthew 7:21-23

Matthew 24:37-39

Matthew 25:31-46

Luke 17:28-30

Romans 6:23

Romans 14:10

1 Corinthians 6:2, 3

2 Peter 2:4

Jude 6

Revelation 15:3

Revelation 19

Revelation 20

Revelation 22:3

Like billions, I want to know.

Know why. Know why a world that knows the giggle of a child also knows the groan of those who've lived too long. Know why so many who claim God's authority are so little like God. Know why people choose to ruin themselves in their quest for personal fulfillment.

I want to know why people make the choices they do. Choices to save or destroy. To put self or Saviour first. I want to know how people find lies so much more appealing than the truth.

And I want to know how the Holy Spirit worked on my grand-father.

Daniel has always been my favorite Bible book. Its title means "God judges," and the book is marked by an interesting duality: The first half tells of Daniel, his three friends, Nebuchadnezzar, and Belshazzar, whom God judges; the second half looks into the prophetic future, with judgment decreed for all humanity.

I grew up loving all of Daniel's tales, yet after my grandfather's death God's long-suffering relationship with Nebuchadnezzar especially intrigued me. Why did God chase so far after that pompous tyrant? To demonstrate the patience He has with even the worst of us, hoping against hope that we'll finally tune in? To show that God won't shut the gate on the world until He has exhausted every way to get our attention?

✦ ✦ ✦

I know my grandfather much better now that he's dead.

My memories of my father's father were of two types: inside and outside.

Inside sitting on his easy chair, a stack of newspapers and a magnifying glass to one side, shelves of short-band radio equipment on the other. On the wall across the room hung a photo of a me I'd long forgotten, clasping my hands and flashing my teeth in a smile while posing with this old man who looked scarcely younger then than he did years later. The rare times I visited and saw the picture, I scarcely knew either man or boy.

Outside sitting on a lawn chair on a sunny day, dogs barking in the background, cats winding their way between the legs of chairs and persons, trees grabbing the sky.

In every memory Grandpa wore black work shoes and blue overalls. He'd carried a cane since he'd irrevocably damaged his side in a boxcar accident as a young man. In the years after, having no high school to attend, he took eighth grade twice, just to learn more. After that he went to work. Perhaps it was just as well—no schools then taught how to be a family man. But he kept a hunger for knowledge.

I knew very little of this. I did know that I'd seen my grandmother at church, but never him. So opposed to Christianity was my grandfather that, trying to hide it, his family was baptized on a Wednesday night.

As long as I'd known, he'd been almost wholly out of our family picture, a raving, shadowed figure.

Out of sight, out of mind. I didn't think to call him Grandpa. He was Elmer Wheeler, nothing more, just words on a page. I chuckled at the story of how he'd filled in "None" for "Middle Name" and gotten mail for Elmer None Wheeler. I thought of my father: Gerald the son of None. I didn't realize that that described my father's feelings precisely.

My dad never thought of his father. A year could go by with scarcely a tinge of memory. Instead he focused on his work, letting little get under his skin. But God's got to start somewhere.

A lot of words cross my father's editing desk. I asked him once what he did with all that information and Christian wisdom, and he claimed that once he'd gone through a book twice as editor, he purged it from memory. One day, though, as he edited a book on intercessory prayer, four words came to his desk, words that wouldn't let go:

"Pray for your father."

"Pray for him?" My father squirmed. "Now? After all these years?"

"Pray for him."

So he told God he didn't know what to ask for. That he'd prayed for so many years with no response. That the Holy Spirit would have to pray for him.

Of course, Grandpa wasn't the only one who needed prayer. We all did—for the Holy Spirit's power to forgive, for our own hearts and attitudes to change. Miracles never happen in a vacuum.

As we prayed, Nana and my uncles noticed little changes. Grandpa's face seemed to soften. He surprised his family with unexpected kindnesses. Some changes, though, you notice only in hindsight. He enjoyed watching television programs on biblical archaeology, an interest my father and I share but had never discussed with him. He no longer watched sports on Saturday afternoons. He wanted someone to pray at dinnertime.

I didn't know any of this, but as I stood at his door for one last visit, I knew that somehow I loved my grandfather again. That was miracle enough for me to keep praying.

I prayed again now. "God, You've changed my heart. You can change his. May he glimpse You through me."

My grandfather welcomed me into his den. As I told him of my present work and studies, I sensed a mood I'd never felt so strongly before. I felt a joy of life that seemed almost surreal. My face cracked into a persistent smile. I felt the Holy Spirit, fresh, heady, and joyous, permeate my personality. I felt fairly dizzy with joy and love.

Grandpa pulled out a new wallet. "Could you use this?" he asked.

"Yeah, I could," I said, pulling my tattered old wallet from my back pocket. "I've needed a new one for a long time. Thank you very much."

"I hope to see you again," Grandpa told me as I left, "if I haven't gone on to the other side."

With a new wallet and a Hershey bar I smiled once more and stepped back outside. My giddiness left me, and peace took its place.

Not long afterward my grandfather lay on his couch, barely able to walk. His life had been plagued by illness, yet somehow he'd survived to age 86. Now his ancient boxcar injury, once treated with heavy X-rays, had grown large and bulged out.

Now he heard a voice in his head.

"Stretch out as long as you can stretch."

Hardly thinking, he obeyed, stretching his legs out straight in front of him.

Then: "Turn your head." As he did, the voice told him precisely the angle to tilt. Then: "Put your two hands over your side where the awful pain is, and *push.*"

He did, positioning his fingers as he was told. As he did so he "saw" into his body—"saw" his ribs and the lump, large, tapered on the ends. And though the pain nearly robbed him of breath, he pushed hard.

He heard a pop, the sound traveling through his body to his head. An intense pain stabbed his side. Then it gradually lessened until he didn't hurt at all.

Awestruck, he lay quietly for a long while. When he heard Nana stirring in the next room, he stood up and went in to see her. "You're not going to believe this," he told her. "You'll think I'm crazy. You're not going to believe this."

One glance at my grandfather was enough to make her believe. He wasn't stooped over with pain. He walked with relative ease, and the gray pallor of his face had brightened to a healthy hue. As he described his experience, he used words she'd never heard him use before—"well educated, like a doctor," she recalled later.

It was an astonishing feat: God healing the lifelong injury of a dying man. Or rather, God healing the bitterness of a man who was slowly coming to life.

Over the next few months my grandfather sometimes seemed preoccupied. "If it's true . . ." Nana heard him ponder to himself more than once. "If it's true . . . I need to know."

The next time I saw Grandpa was in church, a tie around his neck, at rest. According to my grandmother he'd apparently accepted Christ into his heart. I wondered: *Did the look on his face merely reflect the common solemnity of the dead, the expertise of the funeral home, or a greater peacefulness he'd reached?*

The nurse at the hospital had looked at his side and wondered: *What surgery made that perfect scar?*

✦ ✦ ✦

The Bible prophesies a time of answers. A time when the righteous dead are resurrected, and we can begin to heal the damage from generations of sin. A time when the saints will look back over human history, investigating each life to discover how they responded to God's call. A time when unfallen beings from other worlds can examine how sin brought death, and why sinners were worth dying for.

To my questioning mind, this truth speaks to me like no other. God will open the universe's archives to our investigation.

Most pictures I've seen of heaven show barefoot saints kicking back in the shade, petting docile lions, enjoying the company of Christ. And that's all good—but it's only part of the picture. Except for the robes, the pictures rarely suggest judges at work. Yet the Bible tells us we will reign as priests of God.

This judgment will begin to answer all the questions sin leaves us with. How did people make their choices for or against God? Just how did sin claw its way across our history books? We'll trace God's work throughout history, seeing how individual human choices made the difference each time. At long last we will explore the answers for ourselves.

I've lost track of how many times I've read the book of Revelation, yet it still knocks me flat. It's a vast, swirling canvas of stunning symbols: Trumpets. Angels. Horses. Frogs. The sun, moon, and stars. A dragon. The Lion and the Lamb.

For 19 centuries Revelation has boggled the minds of Bible readers. Most find no more meaning in Revelation's icons than in their breakfast bowl of Lucky Charms. As I grew up Adventist, many books and pamphlets promised to decode its mysteries for me. A college professor showed me a key, however, that began to translate those symbols: Plug Revelation into the Bible's 65 other books, for every idea in Revelation is built on the books before it.

In other words, first things first.

I finally understood Revelation as what it says it is in its first verse: "The revelation of Jesus Christ." I discovered the Lamb of God front and center in the book, the One worthy of worship.

And I encountered Revelation's central warning: Beware the liar who imitates the Lamb's every move. Though he deceives many, he will be unmasked as the originator of sin, and be swept away with it. His kingdom of darkness will vanish in the eternal light.

Satan has built his shadow kingdom on lies. For every good thing, Satan offers a counterfeit. For every evil thing, Satan offers an excuse.

While the saved reign in heaven, Satan will be down on earth, where, Revelation tells us, he can deceive no one. He's trapped with only his cohorts and his memories.

✦ ✦ ✦

The final judgment comes as God brings the heavenly city of New Jerusalem to earth. A thousand years of judgment are ended, and God will now wipe the universe clean of sin once and for all.

As God's Holy City lands on earth, God resurrects the lost for a brief moment of time. God will open to them, too, the heavenly records that show how they missed God's gift of eternal life.

The multitude who wanted nothing to do with God at last get their wish. And since nothing can exist without God's power, they are no more.

Sin collapses onto itself. Self-centered at its core, sin devours its crown prince, the father of lies, that old serpent, the devil. Lucifer, the Day-Star who sought his own throne, burns out in the light of God's unshaded glory.

The lake of fire burns out. The universe is finally free of its deadly experiment forever. Free of lies, free of pain. Free to love without fear. Free to enjoy perfect joy. Free to enjoy all that sin promised but could never deliver.

1. What questions do you want to ask God during the millennium?
2. What are Satan's most effective lies?
3. How do you envision heaven?
4. What does it mean to be judged by our works?
5. What excuses keep us from accepting God into our lives?

Tompaul Wheeler, 24, graduated from Southwestern Adventist University with a degree in history and from Andrews University with a degree in God-study. He dabbles in photography and video.

27

THE NEW EARTH
Sam McKee

Why Should I Care?

This world, at best, is a mediocre, half-baked opening band that strives desperately to rouse us for an earthshaking, soul-satisfying concert waiting to burst upon us. The new earth is the climax of the Bible. And whether you know it or not, it's what your soul longs for most.

How Can I Know?

Matthew 5:5	1 Corinthians 13:12
John 14:1-3	Matthew 8:11
Ecclesiastes 3:11	John 17:3
Ephesians 3:20	Hebrews 11:13-16
1 Corinthians 2:9	2 Peter 3:10-13
Isaiah 11:6-9	Revelation 21:1-5
Isaiah 35	Revelation 22:1-6
Jeremiah 29:11-13	

If you could go anywhere in the world to thrill your soul to the core, where would it be?" Paul, an aging but engaging gentleman, asks his young adult friends at a Starbucks coffee shop.

"Dude, I'd go to Vail, Colorado, with my two best friends and surf on three feet of fresh powder on my Burton snowboard . . . slicing and dicing my way through a meadow of trees 10,000 feet up in the sky," says Jake, grinning and turning his eyes back down to his gray Airwalk sneakers.

Jenny's head starts bobbing as she talks. "I'd totally, like, go to the Mall of America in Minnesota, where there are, like, more than 520 specialty stores, not to mention major department stores like Bloomingdale's, Macy's, and Nordstrom. It has almost 50 restaurants, eight nightclubs, 14 movie theater screens, and a million other sights and sounds to dazzle my eyes, empty my purse, and ruin my credit history! Yeah, that's where I'd go, or whatever."

"I'd travel to Europe and visit all the historical sites—the Berlin Wall, the Holocaust memorials—and I'd marvel at the works of Michelangelo," says Naomi, looking thoughtful in her small-rimmed glasses. "I'd also like to sample and savor the sublime medley of ethnic fare in each country."

"No doubt about it," Chris chimes in, wearing a black Nirvana shirt. "I'd organize a music festival and invite the wildest and strangest varieties of bands. I'd have to start with Phish for all my disappointed, disenfranchised Deadhead friends. They'd build the warm community fun feeling. Then Pearl Jam and Creed would bust in for the alternative time. Then, get this, I'd have a rap group—I don't even know any, but they would go next, with a little hip-hop mixed in, too. Switching major gears, I'd pull in Shania Twain, Sarah McLaughlin, and Jewel for my girlfriend to listen to. And all this would happen in my backyard."

Paul laughs and says, "That sounds like an impressive and rare concert, Chris. They're all big names. But almost every concert I've heard of always has some cheesy band that opens for the amazing, heart-thumping, crowd-thrilling premier music experience."

Looking up with his piercing blue eyes, Paul says, "There's a great analogy there for our human experience. This life, at best, is a mediocre, half-baked opening band that strives desperately to rouse us for an earthshaking, soul-satisfying concert that is waiting to burst upon us. That's the climax of the Bible. 'No eye has seen, no ear has heard, no mind has conceived what God has prepared for those who love him' (1 Corinthians 2:9, NIV). The healthy, happy things you love here are a mere spoonful from the ocean of amazement that

God has up His sleeve for the people who set their hearts on Him."

That's the way I think the apostle Paul would share the concept of eternity in a Starbucks coffee shop.

A few years ago I would have been the skeptical one who challenged everything he said. As a young newspaper reporter, I always had a questioning mind to temper my dreamer's heart. I found the same struggle in the writings of an Oxford professor named C. S. Lewis. He struggled for quite some time between faith and doubt, and from this dark struggle came some diamonds of thought. Here's one:

"For we are so little reconciled to time that we are even astonished at it. 'How he's grown,' we exclaim, 'How time flies!' as though the universal form of our experience were again and again a novelty. It is as strange as if a fish were repeatedly surprised at the wetness of water. And that would be strange indeed; unless of course the fish were destined to become, one day, a land animal" (*Reflections on the Psalms* [New York: Harcourt, Brace and Co., 1958], p. 138).

"[God] has also set eternity in the hearts of men; yet they cannot fathom what God has done from beginning to end" (Ecclesiastes 3:11, NIV). We constantly long for eternity as if somewhere, in the deep recesses of our mind, we all know that we were built for it.

Ever been completely shattered by the death of a friend? Ever had your heart broken by someone you cared about? Ever get sick of praying to a God you can't see? Far from denying the Bible, these frustrations only confirm it. The book of Genesis says we were created to be in an environment where we see God face to face when we talk to Him. We were created to be in a world where we don't see our friends or even our pets die. We were created to have perfect unending relationships. Yet we're stuck here on the wrong side of eternity. As my friend Pat Grant says: "We're like a dune buggy stuck in Michigan in the winter." Our tires spin without ceasing. We're frustrated and hungry for more. And we will never be fully satisfied until the original Eden is restored.

The cool part is that Eden will be restored, even renovated. One of the brightest theological reflections I've heard was from a 20-year-old concrete worker/snowboarder. He said, "Sammy, how long did it take God to make this amazing world and all the mountains we snowboard on together?"

"Six days," I said, wondering why he was giving me, the pastor, this Bible trivia quiz.

"When Jesus was leaving this earth, He said, 'I'm going to prepare a place for you.' So how long has He been working on this Paradise?"

"Wow . . . for 2,000 years!" It finally sank in. To think He made this amazing earth, with its cascading waterfalls, leaping dolphins, crashing waves, majestic mountains, and everything else that dazzles my eyes *in six days*. How much more amazing will Paradise be if He's spent 2,000 years dreaming and working on it?

God almost places a bet in the Bible by saying that His eternal vacation will surpass anything we can imagine. Remember, Paul says that no mind has conceived the glories of heaven—and then in Ephesians 3:20, he says, "Now to him who is able to do immeasurably more than all we ask or imagine" (NIV).

If we have some lame view of Paradise with old guys with white robes playing Adventist hymns on golden harps, then God doesn't have to do too much to surpass our low expectations. Instead, I think God wants us to dream about the new earth and long for it and really believe that He has something awesome planned for us.

On this earth we can feel the rush of a raging river on a whitewater rafting adventure. In our urban centers we can go on shopping sprees in huge malls lined with the latest and greatest in fashion and food. Or we can go to Disney World, where the most powerful technology can send us on surreal trips through outer space. All of these incredible things come from puny human minds that only want to make some cash. Now imagine what thrilling plans could come from the infinite mind of God—the God who cared so much about our happiness that He was willing to die for us.

So exercise your faith in God today by dreaming about what you'd like to see or do in the new earth. This is a choose-your-own-adventure, so grab a pen and let's imagine.

Leisure/Sports

You're going to have tons of time. What kinds of things will you want to do for fun?

(Examples: Learn how to play instruments and start a band, explore every corner of creation and paint pictures of nature, ski in 70-degree weather on snow that tastes like Ben & Jerry's ice cream, play basketball at different levels of gravity, shrink down to the size of an ant and explore the land, go sight-seeing with eyes that can zoom to microscopic levels and then scan the distance with more power than a telescope.) Add your own ideas here:

_____

_____

_____

_____

My Mansion

"Let not your heart be troubled: ye believe in God, believe also in me. In my Father's house are many mansions: if it were not so, I would have told you. I go to prepare a place for you. And if I go and prepare a place for you, I will come again, and receive you unto myself; that where I am, there ye may be also" (John 14:1-3).

Jesus is preparing a place for you in the New Jerusalem, but in the new earth it says that we "will build houses and dwell in them" (Isaiah 65:21, NIV). This is your amazing country home:

What will be in your house? (Olympic-size swimming pool, huge aquarium, gingerbread.)

_____

_____

_____

_____

Where will your house be? (In a forest, by a raging river, on a lake.)

_____

_____

_____

Whom will you build it with? (Your dad, Jesus, etc.)

_____

_____

_____

Draw a picture or describe your dream house in the new earth:

_____

_____

_____

_____

People

"Now we see but a poor reflection as in a mirror; then we shall see face to face. Now I know in part; then I shall know fully, even as I am fully known" (1 Corinthians 13:12, NIV). In heaven we will not only recognize people we knew before, but we will have even deeper friendships than ever.

Whom would you like to see in heaven? (Be specific: include people who have passed away, old friends, family, famous people.)

_____

_____

_____

Travel

Adventists have the most positive view of the starlit sky. We believe that those stars are suns in solar systems that haven't broken their connection with the Creator (see the parable of the lost sheep in Luke 15). And those stars are just a tiny sampling of the celestial adventures that await us. One of my favorite authors, Ellen White, described our eternal adventures this way: "All the treasures of the universe will be open to the study of God's redeemed. Unfettered by mortality, they wing their tireless flight to worlds afar. . . . With undimmed vision they gaze upon the glory of creation—suns and stars and systems. . . . One pulse of harmony and gladness beats through the vast creation. From Him who created all, flow life and light and gladness, throughout the realms of illimitable space. From the minutest atom to the greatest world, all things animate and inanimate, in their unshadowed beauty and perfect joy, declare that God is love" (_The Great Controversy_, pp. 677, 678).

Where would you want to travel to in the universe?

_____

_____

_____

Pets

Read Isaiah 11:6-9. Since all animals will be friendly, what kind of pets would you want to have? What would you like to do with them? (Surf on a dolphin's back down a river, use a lion's mane for a pillow.)

_____

_____

_____

_____

Meeting Jesus

We've talked about all the elements of this ultimate party, and now we've come to the most important. Imagine you're standing there in that beautiful place surrounded by all that glory and joy, and you look over and see Jesus. You look down and see the scars in His hands, and you realize that He left all this beauty to come to your broken world to save you. He's the one who died for you, He's the one who invited you, and He's the one who's carried you to this place.

What will you say to Him?

_____

_____

_____

_____

What would you want to do for (or with) Him?

_____

_____

_____

_____

Million-Dollar Question

How can you be sure you're going to heaven?

"Now this is eternal life: that they may know you, the one true God, and Jesus Christ, whom you have sent" (John 17:3). Your assurance of eternal life won't be found in your good deeds, your head knowledge, or your church attendance. Salvation is found in an intimate, personal connection. It's in knowing Jesus as your older brother, your best friend, your Creator and Saviour—the one who picks you up every time you fall, and the one training you step by step for spiritual excellence. If you're going to a party, the best preparation is to get to know the host.

When you hear Jesus calling you to reach your world, He's simply asking you to invite people to the ultimate party. Show them the directions to get there (in the Bible), and help them get to know the Host (Jesus).

One of your greatest joys in Paradise will be seeing people there because of the way you shared God's love with them on earth. You've got all eternity to explore creation, to sing God's praise, and to marvel at His Word. But now is the only time in the history of the universe you'll ever have the chance to help God when His heart is on the line. Now is the only time we can reach out to God's lost children and love them back into His arms.

So Christianity begins and ends with the mission. Christ's mission started it, and your mission will finish it. By the way you live and the way you love, you can become an invitation to the place that every human longs for. The best way to start your mission is to pick three people who don't know God and make this promise:

I will daily lift these people into God's arms, praying with confidence that He will bless every part of their lives and use me in any and every way possible to lead them to Christ and His salvation:

_____

_____

_____

_____

Sam McKee, 25, lives in Colorado Springs, Colorado, where he laughs, prays, and plays with the greatest kids in the world at the Central Seventh-day Adventist Church. He enjoys being a youth pastor, snowboarding, playing guitar, and inviting people to heaven.

APPENDIX _____

1. The Holy Scriptures.

The Holy Scriptures, Old and New Testaments, are the written Word of God, given by divine inspiration through holy men of God who spoke and wrote as they were moved by the Holy Spirit. In this Word, God has committed to man the knowledge necessary for salvation. The Holy Scriptures are the infallible revelation of His will. They are the standard of character, the test of experience, the authoritative revealer of doctrines, and the trustworthy record of God's acts in history. (2 Peter 1:20, 21; 2 Timothy 3:16, 17; Psalm 119:105; Proverbs 30:5, 6; Isaiah 8:20; John 17:17; 1 Thessalonians 2:13; Hebrews 4:12.)

2. The Trinity.

There is one God: Father, Son, and Holy Spirit, a unity of three co-eternal Persons. God is immortal, all-powerful, all-knowing, above all, and ever present. He is infinite and beyond human comprehension, yet known through His self-revelation. He is forever worthy of worship, adoration, and service by the whole creation. (Deuteronomy 6:4; Matthew 28:19; 2 Corinthians 13:14; Ephesians 4:4-6; 1 Peter 1:2; 1 Timothy 1:17; Revelation 14:7.)

3. The Father.

God the Eternal Father is the Creator, Source, Sustainer, and Sovereign of all creation. He is just and holy, merciful and gracious, slow to anger, and abounding in steadfast love and faithfulness. The qualities and powers exhibited in the Son and the Holy Spirit are also revelations of the Father. (Genesis 1:1; Revelation 4:11; 1 Corinthians 15:28; John 3:16; 1 John 4:8; 1 Timothy 1:17; Exodus 34:6, 7; John 14:9.)

4. The Son.

God the eternal Son became incarnate in Jesus Christ. Through Him all things were created, the character of God is revealed, the salvation of humanity is accomplished, and the world is judged. Forever truly God, He became also truly man, Jesus the Christ. He was conceived of the Holy Spirit and born of the virgin Mary. He lived and experienced temptation as a human being, but perfectly exemplified the righteousness and love of God. By His miracles He manifested God's power and was attested as God's promised Messiah. He suffered and died voluntarily on the cross for our sins and in our place, was raised from the dead, and ascended to minister in the heavenly sanctuary in our behalf. He will come again in glory for the final deliverance of His people and the restoration of all things. (John 1:1-3, 14; Colossians 1:15-19; John 10:30; 14:9; Romans 6:23; 2 Corinthians 5:17-19; John 5:22; Luke 1:35; Philippians 2:5-11; Hebrews 2:9-18; 1 Corinthians 15:3, 4; Hebrews 8:1, 2; John 14:1-3.)

5. The Holy Spirit.

God the eternal Spirit was active with the Father and the Son in Creation, incarnation, and redemption. He inspired the writers of Scripture. He filled Christ's life with power. He draws and convicts human beings; and those who respond He renews and transforms into the image of God. Sent by the Father and the Son to be always with His children, He extends spiritual gifts to the church, empowers it to bear witness to Christ, and in harmony with the Scriptures leads it into all truth. (Genesis 1:1, 2; Luke 1:35; 4:18; Acts 10:38; 2 Peter 1:21; 2 Corinthians 3:18; Ephesians 4:11, 12; Acts 1:8; John 14:16-18, 26; 15:26, 27; 16:7-13.)

6. Creation.

God is Creator of all things, and has revealed in Scripture the authentic account of His creative activity. In six days the Lord made "the heaven and the earth" and all living things upon the earth, and rested on the seventh day of that first week. Thus He established the Sabbath as a perpetual memorial of His completed creative work. The first man and woman were made in the image of God as the crowning work of Creation, given dominion over the world, and charged with responsibility to care for it. When the world was finished it was "very good," declaring the glory of God. (Genesis 1; 2; Exodus 20:8-11; Psalm 19:1-6; 33:6, 9; 104; Hebrews 11:3.)

7. The Nature of Man.

Man and woman were made in the image of God with individuality, the power and freedom to think and to do. Though created free beings, each is an indivisible unity of body, mind, and spirit, dependent upon God for life and breath and all else. When our first parents disobeyed God, they denied their dependence upon Him and fell from their high position under God. The image of God in them was marred and they became subject to death. Their descendants share this fallen nature and its consequences. They are born with weaknesses and tendencies to evil. But God in Christ reconciled the world to Himself and by His Spirit restores in penitent mortals the image of their Maker. Created for the glory of God, they are called to love Him and one another, and to care for their environment. (Genesis 1:26-28; 2:7; Psalm 8:4-8; Acts 17:24-28; Genesis 3; Psalm 51:5; Romans 5:12-17; 2 Corinthians 5:19, 20; Psalm 51:10; 1 John 4:7, 8, 11, 20; Genesis 2:15.)

8. The Great Controversy.

All humanity is now involved in a great controversy between Christ and Satan regarding the character of God, His law, and His sovereignty over the universe. This conflict originated in heaven when a created being, endowed with freedom of choice, in self-exaltation became Satan, God's adversary, and led into rebellion a portion of the angels. He introduced the spirit of rebellion into this world when he led Adam and Eve into sin. This human sin resulted in the distortion of the image of God in humanity, the disordering of the created world, and its eventual devastation at the time of the worldwide flood. Observed by the whole creation, this world became the arena of the universal conflict, out of which the God of love will ultimately be vindicated. To assist His people in this controversy, Christ sends the Holy Spirit and the loyal angels to guide, protect, and sustain them in the way of salvation. (Revelation 12:4-9; Isaiah 14:12-14; Ezekiel 28:12-18; Genesis 3; Romans 1:19-32; 5:12-21; 8:19-22; Genesis 6-8; 2 Peter 3:6; 1 Corinthians 4:9; Hebrews 1:14.)

9. The Life, Death, and Resurrection of Christ.

In Christ's life of perfect obedience to God's will, His suffering, death, and resurrection, God provided the only means of atonement for human sin, so that those who by faith accept this atonement may have eternal life, and the whole creation may better understand the infinite and holy love of the Creator. This perfect atonement vindicates the righteousness of God's law and the graciousness of His character; for it both condemns our sin and provides for our forgiveness. The death of Christ is substitutionary and expiatory, reconciling and transforming. The resurrection of Christ proclaims God's triumph over the forces of evil, and for those who accept the atonement assures their final victory over sin and death. It declares the Lordship of Jesus Christ, before whom every knee in heaven and on earth will bow. (John 3:16; Isaiah 53; 1 Peter 2:21, 22; 1 Corinthians 15:3, 4, 20-22; 2 Corinthians 5:14, 15, 19-21; Romans 1:4; 3:25; 4:25; 8:3, 4; 1 John 2:2; 4:10; Colossians 2:15; Philippians 2:6-11.)

10. The Experience of Salvation.

In infinite love and mercy God made Christ, who knew no sin, to be sin for us, so that in Him we might be made the righteousness of God. Led by the Holy Spirit we sense our need, acknowledge our sinfulness, repent of our transgressions, and exercise faith in Jesus as Lord and Christ, as Substitute and Example. This faith which receives salvation comes through the divine power of the Word and is the gift of God's grace. Through Christ we are justified, adopted as

God's sons and daughters, and delivered from the lordship of sin. Through the Spirit we are born again and sanctified; the Spirit renews our minds, writes God's law of love in our hearts, and we are given the power to live a holy life. Abiding in Him we become partakers of the divine nature and have the assurance of salvation now and in the judgment. (2 Corinthians 5:17-21; John 3:16; Galatians 1:4; 4:4-7; Titus 3:3-7; John 16:8; Galatians 3:13, 14; 1 Peter 2:21, 22; Romans 10:17; Luke 17:5; Mark 9:23, 24; Ephesians 2:5-10; Romans 3:21-26; Colossians 1:13, 14; Romans 8:14-17; Galatians 3:26; John 3:3-8; 1 Peter 1:23; Romans 12:2; Hebrews 8:7-12; Ezekiel 36:25-27; 2 Peter 1:3, 4; Romans 8:1-4; 5:6-10.)

11. The Church.

The church is the community of believers who confess Jesus Christ as Lord and Savior. In continuity with the people of God in Old Testament times, we are called out from the world; and we join together for worship, for fellowship, for instruction in the Word, for the celebration of the Lord's Supper, for service to all mankind, and for the worldwide proclamation of the gospel. The church derives its authority from Christ, who is the incarnate Word, and from the Scriptures, which are the written Word. The church is God's family; adopted by Him as children, its members live on the basis of the new covenant. The church is the body of Christ, a community of faith of which Christ Himself is the Head. The church is the bride for whom Christ died that He might sanctify and cleanse her. At His return in triumph, He will present her to Himself a glorious church, the faithful of all the ages, the purchase of His blood, not having spot or wrinkle, but holy and without blemish. (Genesis 12:3; Acts 7:38; Ephesians 4:11-15; 3:8-11; Matthew 28:19, 20; 16:13-20; 18:18; Ephesians 2:19-22; 1:22, 23; 5:23-27; Colossians 1:17, 18.)

12. The Remnant and Its Mission.

The universal church is composed of all who truly believe in Christ, but in the last days, a time of widespread apostasy, a remnant has been called out to keep the commandments of God and the faith of Jesus. This remnant announces the arrival of the judgment hour, proclaims salvation through Christ, and heralds the approach of His second advent. This proclamation is symbolized by the three angels of Revelation 14; it coincides with the work of judgment in heaven and results in a work of repentance and reform on earth. Every believer is called to have a personal part in this worldwide witness. (Revelation 12:17; 14:6-12; 18:1-4; 2 Corinthians 5:10; Jude 3, 14; 1 Peter 1:16-19; 2 Peter 3:10-14; Revelation 21:1-14.)

13. Unity in the Body of Christ.

The church is one body with many members, called from every nation, kindred, tongue, and people. In Christ we are a new creation; distinctions of race, culture, learning, and nationality, and differences between high and low, rich and poor, male and female, must not be divisive among us. We are all equal in Christ, who by one Spirit has bonded us into one fellowship with Him and with one another; we are to serve and be served without partiality or reservation. Through the revelation of Jesus Christ in the Scriptures we share the same faith and hope, and reach out in one witness to all. This unity has its source in the oneness of the triune God, who has adopted us as His children. (Romans 12:4, 5; 1 Corinthians 12:12-14; Matthew 28:19, 20; Psalm 133:1; 2 Corinthians 5:16, 17; Acts 17:26, 27; Galatians 3:27, 29; Colossians 3:10-15; Ephesians 4:14-16; 4:1-6; John 17:20-23.)

14. Baptism.

By baptism we confess our faith in the death and resurrection of Jesus Christ, and testify of our death to sin and of our purpose to walk in newness of life. Thus we acknowledge Christ as Lord and Saviour, become His people, and are received as members by His church. Baptism is a symbol of our union with Christ, the forgiveness of our sins, and our reception of the Holy Spirit. It is by immersion in water and is contingent on an affirmation of faith in Jesus and evidence of repentance of sin. It follows instruction in the Holy Scriptures and acceptance of their teachings. (Romans 6:1-6; Colossians 2:12, 13; Acts 16:30-33; 22:16; 2:38; Matthew 28:19, 20.)

15. The Lord's Supper.

The Lord's Supper is a participation in the emblems of the body and blood of Jesus as an expression of faith in Him, our Lord and Saviour. In this experience of communion Christ is present to meet and strengthen His people. As we partake, we joyfully proclaim the Lord's death until He comes again. Preparation for the Supper includes self-examination, repentance, and confession. The Master ordained the service of foot washing to signify renewed cleansing, to express a willingness to serve one another in Christlike humility, and to unite our hearts in love. The Communion service is open to all believing Christians. (1 Corinthians 10:16, 17; 11:23-30; Matthew 26:17-30; Revelation 3:20; John 6:48-63; 13:1-17.)

16. Spiritual Gifts and Ministries.

God bestows upon all members of His church in every age spiritual gifts which each member is to employ in loving ministry for the common good of the church and of humanity. Given by the agency of the Holy Spirit, who apportions to each member as He wills, the gifts provide all abilities and ministries needed by the church to fulfill its divinely ordained functions. According to the Scriptures, these gifts include such ministries as faith, healing, prophecy, proclamation, teaching, administration, reconciliation, compassion, and self-sacrificing service and charity for the help and encouragement of people. Some members are called of God and endowed by the Spirit for functions recognized by the church in pastoral, evangelistic, apostolic, and teaching ministries particularly needed to equip the members for service, to build up the church to spiritual maturity, and to foster unity of the faith and knowledge of God. When members employ these spiritual gifts as faithful stewards of God's varied grace, the church is protected from the destructive influence of false doctrine, grows with a growth that is from God, and is built up in faith and love. (Romans 12:4-8; 1 Corinthians 12:9-11, 27, 28; Ephesians 4:8, 11-16; Acts 6:1-7; 1 Timothy 3:1-13; 1 Peter 4:10, 11.)

17. The Gift of Prophecy.

One of the gifts of the Holy Spirit is prophecy. This gift is an identifying mark of the remnant church and was manifested in the ministry of Ellen. G. White. As the Lord's messenger, her writings are a continuing and authoritative source of truth which provide for the church comfort, guidance, instruction, and correction. They also make clear that the Bible is the standard by which all teaching and experience must be tested. (Joel 2:28, 29; Acts 2:14-21; Hebrews 1:1-3; Revelation 12:17; 19:10.)

18. The Law of God.

The great principles of God's law are embodied in the Ten Commandments and exemplified in the life of Christ. They express God's love, will, and purposes concerning human conduct and relationships and are binding upon all people in every age. These precepts are the basis of God's covenant with His people and the standard in God's judgment. Through the agency of the Holy Spirit they point out sin and awaken a sense of need for a Saviour. Salvation is all of grace and not of works, but its fruitage is obedience to the Commandments. This obedience develops Christian character and results in a sense of well-being. It is an evidence of our love for the Lord and our concern for our fellow men. The obedience of faith demonstrates the power of Christ to transform lives, and therefore strengthens Christian witness. (Exodus 20:1-17; Psalm 40:7, 8; Matthew 22:36-40; Deuteronomy 28:1-14; Matthew 5:17-20; Hebrews 8:8-10; John 15:7-10; Ephesians 2:8-10; 1 John 5:3; Romans 8:3, 4; Psalm 19:7-14.)

19. The Sabbath.

The beneficent Creator, after the six days of Creation, rested on the seventh day and instituted the Sabbath for all people as a memorial of Creation. The fourth commandment of God's unchangeable law requires the observance of this seventh-day Sabbath as the day of rest, worship, and ministry in harmony with the teaching and practice of Jesus, the Lord of the Sabbath. The Sabbath is a day of delightful communion with God and one another. It is a symbol of our redemption in Christ, a sign of our sanctification, a token of our allegiance, and a foretaste of our eternal future in God's kingdom. The Sabbath is God's perpetual sign of His eternal covenant between Him and His people. Joyful observance of this holy time from evening to evening, sunset to sunset, is a celebration of God's creative and redemptive acts. (Genesis 2:1-3; Exodus 20:8-11; Luke 4:16; Isaiah 56:5, 6; 58:13, 14; Matthew 12:1-12; Exodus 31:13-17; Ezekiel 20:12, 20; Deuteronomy 5:12-15; Hebrews 4:1-11; Leviticus 23:32; Mark 1:32.)

20. Stewardship.

We are God's stewards, entrusted by Him with time and opportunities, abilities and possessions, and the blessings of the earth and its resources. We are responsible to Him for their proper use. We acknowledge God's ownership by faithful service to Him and our fellow men, and by returning tithes and giving offerings for the proclamation of His gospel and the support and growth of His church. Stewardship is a privilege given to us by God for nurture in love and the victory over selfishness and covetousness. The steward rejoices in the blessings that come to others as a result of his faithfulness. (Genesis 1:26-28; 2:15; 1 Chronicles 29:14; Haggai 1:3-11; Malachi 3:8-12; 1 Corinthians 9:9-14; Matthew 23:23; 2 Corinthians 8:1-15; Romans 15:26, 27.)

21. Christian Behavior.

We are called to be a godly people who think, feel, and act in harmony with the principles of heaven. For the Spirit to recreate in us the character of our Lord we involve ourselves only in those things which will produce Christlike purity, health, and joy in our lives. This means that our amusement and entertainment should meet the highest standards of Christian taste and beauty. While recognizing cultural differences, our dress is to be simple, modest, and neat, befitting those whose true beauty does not consist of outward adornment but in the imperishable ornament of a gentle and quiet spirit. It also means that because our bodies are the temples of the Holy Spirit, we are to care for them intelligently. Along with adequate exercise and rest, we are to adopt the most healthful diet possible and abstain from the unclean foods identified in the Scriptures. Since alcoholic beverages, tobacco, and the irresponsible use of drugs and narcotics are harmful to our bodies, we are to abstain from them as well. Instead, we are to engage in whatever brings our thoughts and bodies into the discipline of Christ, who desires our wholesomeness, joy, and goodness. (Romans 12:1, 2; 1 John 2:6; Ephesians 5:1-21; Philippians 4:8; 2 Corinthians 10:5; 6:14-7:1; 1 Peter 3:1-4; 1 Corinthians 6:19, 20; 10:31; Leviticus 11:1-47; 3 John 2.)

22. Marriage and the Family.

Marriage was divinely established in Eden and affirmed by Jesus to be a lifelong union between a man and a woman in loving companionship. For the Christian a marriage commitment is to God as well as to the spouse, and should be entered into only between partners who share a common faith. Mutual love, honor, respect, and responsibility are the fabric of this relationship, which is to reflect the love, sanctity, closeness, and permanence of the relationship between Christ and His church. Regarding divorce, Jesus taught that the person who divorces a spouse, except for fornication, and marries another, commits adultery. Although some family relationships may fall short of the ideal, marriage partners who fully commit themselves to each other in Christ may achieve loving unity through the guidance of the Spirit and the nurture of the church. God blesses the family and intends that its members shall assist each other toward complete maturity. Parents are to bring up their children to love and obey the Lord. By their example and their words they are to teach them that Christ is a loving disciplinarian, ever tender and caring, who wants them to become members of His body, the family of God. Increasing family closeness is one of the earmarks of the final gospel message. (Genesis 2:18-25; Matthew 19:3-9; John 2:1-11; 2 Corinthians 6:14; Ephesians 5:21-33; Matthew 5:31, 32; Mark 10:11, 12; Luke 16:18; 1 Corinthians 7:10, 11; Exodus 20:12; Ephesians 6:1-4; Deuteronomy 6:5-9; Proverbs 22:6; Malachi 4:5, 6.)

23. Christ's Ministry in the Heavenly Sanctuary.

There is a sanctuary in heaven, the true tabernacle which the Lord set up and not man. In it Christ ministers on our behalf, making available to believers the benefits of His atoning sacrifice offered once for all on the cross. He was inaugurated as our great High Priest and began His intercessory ministry at the time of His ascension. In 1844, at the end of the prophetic period of 2300 days, He entered the second and last phase of His atoning ministry. It is a work of investigative judgment which is part of the ultimate disposition of all sin, typified by the cleansing of the ancient Hebrew sanctuary on the Day of Atonement. In that typical service the sanctuary was cleansed with the blood of animal sacrifices, but the heavenly things are purified with the perfect sacrifice of the blood of Jesus. The investigative judgment reveals to heavenly intelligences who among the dead are asleep in Christ and therefore, in Him, are deemed worthy to have part in the first resurrection. It also makes manifest who among the living are abiding in Christ, keeping the commandments of God and the faith of Jesus, and in Him, therefore, are ready for translation into His everlasting kingdom. This judgment vindicates the justice of God in saving those who believe in Jesus. It declares that those who have remained loyal to God shall receive the kingdom. The completion of this ministry of Christ will mark the close of human probation before the Second Advent. (Hebrews 8:1-5; 4:14-16; 9:11-28; 10:19-22; 1:3; 2:16, 17; Daniel 7:9-27; 8:13, 14; 9:24-27; Numbers 14:34; Ezekiel 4:6; Leviticus 16; Revelation 14:6, 7; 20:12; 14:12; 22:12.)

24. The Second Coming of Christ.

The second coming of Christ is the blessed hope of the church, the grand climax of the gospel. The Saviour's coming will be literal, personal, visible, and worldwide. When He returns, the righteous dead will be resurrected, and together with the righteous living will be glorified and taken to heaven, but the unrighteous will die. The almost complete fulfillment of most lines of prophecy, together with the present condition of the world, indicates that Christ's coming is imminent. The time of that event has not been revealed, and we are therefore exhorted to be ready at all times. (Titus 2:13; Hebrews 9:28; John 14:1-3; Acts 1:9-11; Matthew 24:14; Revelation 1:7; Matthew 24:43, 44; 1 Thessalonians 4:13-18; 1 Corinthians 15:51-54; 2 Thessalonians 1:7-10; 2:8; Revelation 14:14-20; 19:11-21; Matthew 24; Mark 13; Luke 21; 2 Timothy 3:1-5; 1 Thessalonians 5:1-6.)

25. Death and Resurrection.

The wages of sin is death. But God, who alone is immortal, will grant eternal life to His redeemed. Until that day death is an unconscious state for all people. When Christ, who is our life, appears, the resurrected righteous and the living righteous will be glorified and caught up to meet their Lord. The second resurrection, the resurrection of the unrighteous, will take place a thousand years later. (Romans 6:23; 1 Timothy 6:15, 16; Ecclesiastes 9:5, 6; Psalm 146:3, 4; John 11:11-14; Colossians 3:4; 1 Corinthians 15:51-54; 1 Thessalonians 4:13-17; John 5:28, 29; Revelation 20:1-10.)

26. The Millennium and the End of Sin.

The millennium is the thousand-year reign of Christ with His saints in heaven between the first and second resurrections. During this time the wicked dead will be judged; the earth will be utterly desolate, without living human inhabitants, but occupied by Satan and his angels. At its close Christ with His saints and the Holy City will descend from heaven to earth. The unrighteous dead will then be resurrected, and with Satan and his angels will surround the city;

but fire from God will consume them and cleanse the earth. The universe will thus be freed of sin and sinners forever. (Revelation 20; 1 Corinthians 6:2, 3; Jeremiah 4:23-26; Revelation 21:1-5; Malachi 4:1; Ezekiel 28:18, 19.)

27. The New Earth.

On the new earth, in which righteousness dwells, God will provide an eternal home for the redeemed and a perfect environment for everlasting life, love, joy, and learning in His presence. For here God Himself will dwell with His people, and suffering and death will have passed away. The great controversy will be ended, and sin will be no more. All things, animate and inanimate, will declare that God is love; and He shall reign forever. Amen. (2 Peter 3:13; Isaiah 35; 65:17-25; Matthew 5:5; Revelation 21:1-7; 22:1-5; 11:15.)